# 1812

# 1812

## A Traveler's Guide

### TO THE WAR THAT DEFINED A CONTINENT

NATIONAL GEOGRAPHIC

WASHINGTON, D.C.

# CONTENTS

Previous pages: Sackets Harbor Battlefield State Historic Site, Lake Ontario; left: raising the flag at Fort George, Niagara; above: cannon at Fort Mackinac; right: pistol used by U.S. Gen. James Winchester at the Battle of the River Raisin; top right: button from the dress coat of the British 49th Regiment of Foot

## »*A note from Parks Canada*

A fort destroyed in a devastating bombardment, battlefields where foreign invaders were turned back, the stone ramparts of the most formidable fortification in North America, sites where Canadian heroes died in desperate battles: Such unforgettable places where the drama of the War of 1812 unfolded are preserved by Parks Canada—for the people of Canada and the enjoyment of all.

From Newfoundland to the far Great Lakes, Parks Canada tells the stories of the War of 1812 at a network of national historic sites commemorating this nation-building era. These special places attract and reward visitors of all ages. Whether it is family life, live music, or the crack and thunder of muskets and cannon, the past becomes vividly present. Our treasured national historic sites are exciting, inspiring, and fascinating to visit.

The War of 1812 is extremely significant in Canadian history. When the very existence of British North America was threatened, a small band of British professional soldiers and sailors, French- and English-speaking volunteer militia, and aboriginal allies came together to stand guard and successfully defend their land and its waterways, ensuring a future for Canada as an independent nation with its own values and traditions.

The national historic sites of Canada are proud treasures where our rich heritage is cherished and celebrated. The welcoming Parks Canada team invites visitors to be enriched by personally experiencing these places to discover, to reflect, to enjoy, and to connect with the captivating stories of those who came before us.

Enemies long ago, Canada and the United States now share a deep and abiding friendship built on trust and respect. This guidebook, a two-nation publication, is emblematic of the spirit of friendship and collaboration between our countries, the wise legacy of the War of 1812. I hope it will help you to appreciate the lessons of conflict and to celebrate the results of two centuries of peace and mutual understanding.

—ALAN LATOURELLE, *CEO, Parks Canada*

# ≫*A note from the National Park Service*

**P**erhaps the least known war in American history—fought for obscure reasons, largely along the nation's frontier—the War of 1812 was a small war, but with far-reaching consequences. As Benjamin Franklin said at the end of the American Revolution, "The war of revolution is won, but the war for independence is yet to be fought." By 1812, the United States was a young republic, striving and ambitious, while in Canada the global British Empire still had interests in North America.

Angered by British interference in its commerce and the impressment of American sailors, the United States declared war and invaded British Canada. The fighting lasted for nearly three years, giving birth to such American icons as "Old Ironsides" and "The Star-Spangled Banner." The reality behind this often glorified history is as complicated as today's current events: There was intense disagreement over the war with Britain; to many it was an ill-conceived land grab, whereas others saw it as necessary to protect American rights and fulfill the legacy of the Revolution. For the British and their subjects in Canada it was defense against American aggression, while for Native Americans it was a fight for survival.

In the end, no territory changed hands, but the war produced a stronger national unity and identity. The end of the War of 1812 ushered in an era of enduring peace between the Euro-American combatants but led to the tragic policies toward Native Americans in the interests of westward expansion.

Commemorating the 200th anniversary of the War of 1812, we find ourselves asking questions that were not only current then but are also current now: What does it mean to be American? How do we ensure that this experiment in democracy lives on? The 200-year-old questions of sovereignty, national interests, foreign policy, even civil rights echo forward from 1812. Viewed in this light, it does not seem like such an obscure event.

In collaboration with Parks Canada, the Lake Champlain Basin Program, and other partners, the National Park Service is proud to present this guide. The authenticity of place is what makes parks and historic sites such powerful sources not only of education but also of self-discovery. On behalf of the National Park Service, it is an honor to serve as the steward of our collective heritage and the wisdom it contains.

—JONATHAN B. JARVIS, *Director, National Park Service*

# ABOUT THIS BOOK

**P**ublished to mark the 200th anniversary of the War of 1812, *1812: A Traveler's Guide* brings together places in the United States and Canada that are connected with the war. These include towns, battle sites, forts, navy yards, cemeteries, and the historic trails of the British and U.S. troops as they marched to battle. Developed with the help of Parks Canada, the U.S. National Park Service, the Champlain Valley National Heritage Partnership, and staff at each of the sites, this guide relates the struggles of both sides, honors the men who fought, and details the many ways in which the sites commemorate the history today, with living history displays and reenactments.

The six chapters of this book reflect the main theaters: Old Northwest; Niagara Region; Lake Ontario; St. Lawrence River, Lake Champlain, and Richelieu Valley; Atlantic Seaboard; and Southeast. Sites are arranged geographically within each chapter.

The address, website, and phone number of each site appear at the bottom of the description, along with days or months when a site is closed (though not public holidays); a dollar sign indicates there is an entrance fee.

The book frequently uses the terms Upper and Lower Canada. In the early 19th century, eastern Canada comprised English-speaking Upper Canada (modern Ontario) and mainly French-speaking Lower Canada (modern Quebec). For the purposes of this guide, the term Native Nations refers to all Native peoples of North America—known as Native Americans or American Indians in the U.S. and First Nations in Canada.

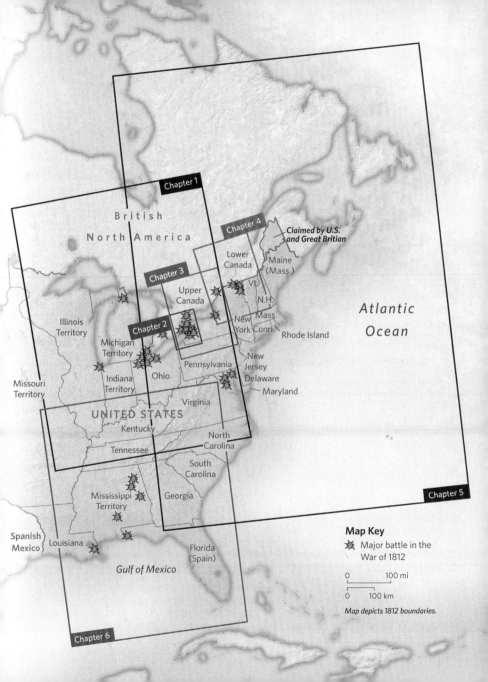

British
North America

Chapter 1

Chapter 3

Chapter 4

Lower
Canada

Upper
Canada

Maine
(Mass.)

Claimed by U.S.
and Great Britian

Vt.

Chapter 2

N.H.

Mass.

New
York

Conn.

Rhode Island

Atlantic
Ocean

Illinois
Territory

Michigan
Territory

Indiana
Territory

Ohio

Pennsylvania

New
Jersey

Delaware

Maryland

Missouri
Territory

UNITED STATES

Virginia

Kentucky

Tennessee

North
Carolina

South
Carolina

Mississippi
Territory

Georgia

Spanish
Mexico

Louisiana

Florida
(Spain)

Gulf of Mexico

Chapter 5

Chapter 6

### Map Key

✳ Major battle in the
War of 1812

0      100 mi

0      100 km

*Map depicts 1812 boundaries.*

# *INTRODUCTION*

**O**n June 18, 1812, the United States of America declared war on the United Kingdom of Great Britain and Ireland and its possessions. For almost a thousand days, American and British forces and their Native allies fought across eastern North America from the Gulf of Mexico to the northern Great Lakes; from the Mississippi Valley to the Atlantic seaboard; and on the Atlantic, Pacific, and Indian Oceans.

The Treaty of Ghent in December 1814 ended what would be the last Anglo-American war. At the peace negotiations in Belgium both sides agreed to return land captured during the war and to settle future boundary disputes by a joint committee. While the question of who won the war continues to be debated on both sides of the border, many Canadians and Americans will firmly state that their ancestors won the War of 1812.

**The first important naval battle of the war took place on August 19, 1812, when U.S.S. *Constitution* dismasted the British warship, H.M.S. *Guerriere*. This resounding U.S. success lifted morale on the American side and proved that British naval power, the strongest in the world at the time, was not invincible.**

The war left a profound and lasting impression on all of the participants and on the North American continent, transforming political landscapes and cultural imaginations. While it helped to define the nascent American republic as a unified, sovereign nation and contributed to the formation of Canada in 1867, it also intensified the desperate struggles of Native Nations in defense of their homelands. Peace and plenty remained elusive goals for many.

## Causes of the War of 1812

The United States' declaration of war on Great Britain cited a list of grievances. They included the Royal Navy's enforcement of Orders in Council limiting trade with Europe, and the practice of "impressment" by which the British forcibly removed purportedly British-born sailors from U.S. ships for service on British warships.

Both policies were critical to Britain's effort to maximize its naval power in its ongoing war with France, which escalated after Napoleon Bonaparte assumed the title of Emperor of the French in 1804.

From the American perspective, Britain's strategy was an affront to the new republic's national sovereignty that fueled war fever. Unable to contemplate an invasion of Britain itself, the United States' only alternative was to strike at Britain's North American provinces (now Canada) and use territorial conquests to secure concessions on maritime issues. The conquest of most of Canada was expected to be, in the words of Thomas Jefferson, "a mere matter of marching."

Some Americans, especially in the West, were eager to target Canada for another reason: They hoped to drive Britain from North America, eliminate a powerful rival, and put an end to perceived British influence over indigenous peoples. Annexation of British North America was the goal for many Americans although not official policy.

The Treaty of Paris that granted the United States independence in 1783 gave the new republic the vast lands between the Appalachian Mountains and the Mississippi River. Within two decades, the United States also amassed territories west of the Mississippi through the Louisiana Purchase from France. These lands were the homelands of many Native Nations.

Land speculators and settlers who pushed west met with resistance to these encroachments. A confederation of members of various Native Nations, inspired by the Shawnee "Prophet" Tenskwatawa and united through the political acumen of his brother Tecumseh, convened at Prophetstown, in Indiana Territory. Frontier tensions increased as settlers and Native warriors clashed. The confederation grew as a tireless Tecumseh traveled from the British North American border to the far south speaking of the need for all tribes to unite to fight the common foe. In November 1811, while Tecumseh pursued alliances in Creek and Choctaw territories, Indiana Governor William Henry Harrison led a force against the confederation at the Battle of Tippecanoe and burned Prophetstown after the confederation warriors retreated.

### 1812: A Mere Matter of Marching

When war broke out, British North America was in dire straits. Locked in a death struggle on the European continent, Britain could spare few professional troops to defend British North America and needed militia volunteers to supplement the small army

### Key Dates 1812

✳ **June 18** U.S. declares war

✳ **August 16** British capture Detroit

✳ **October 13** Battle of Queenston Heights

✳ **October 25** U.S.S. *United States* v. H.M.S. *Macedonian*

✳ **December 29** U.S.S. *Constitution* v. H.M.S. *Java*

guarding the vast North American territory. They also needed help from a number of Native Nations. Britain sought to defend British North America while hoping to end the war through negotiation, at least until victories in Europe freed up more resources.

The Americans planned to launch a three-pronged assault against the British. From Detroit an army would invade Upper Canada, capturing the Royal Navy's Lake Erie headquarters and the British Indian Department complex at Amherstburg. In a second campaign, the Americans planned to assemble an army on the Niagara frontier and invade along the Niagara River, establishing a bridgehead for the conquest of the western half of Upper Canada and its provincial capital at York (Toronto) in the following year. In the final phase they would attack Montreal and seize control of Lower Canada.

**Initial invasions** U.S. Brig. Gen. William Hull launched the first invasion, crossing the Detroit River to occupy Sandwich on July 12, 1812. Hull's plan, to attack Fort Amherstburg, fell apart when the British and Native allies stopped his army twice at the Canard River between

**The Shawnee leader Tecumseh led a Native confederation allied to the British.**

Sandwich and Amherstburg. Elsewhere, the British commander of Fort St. Joseph near Sault Ste. Marie learned of the declaration of war before his American counterparts at nearby Fort Mackinac. He led a force of regulars, Canadian militia, and Native and Métis allies that forced the Americans to surrender the fort without a shot fired. On learning the news Hull returned to Detroit and abandoned U.S. designs along the Detroit frontier for the rest of the year.

At Fort George in Niagara (now Niagara-on-the-Lake) Maj. Gen. Sir Isaac Brock, administrator and military commander of Upper Canada, sought to strengthen British alliances with Native groups with an early victory over the Americans. He and Tecumseh met at Amherstburg and planned a daring attack on Detroit. Brock and his small army of British regulars, militia volunteers, and Native allies bluffed Hull into surrendering his superior forces at Detroit and, with that, the entire Michigan Territory.

In October, a U.S. force invaded Upper Canada at Queenston on the Niagara frontier but was defeated by British and Canadian troops and Native warriors. During the Battle of Queenston Heights, Brock was killed leading his troops.

Meanwhile, Maj. Gen. Henry Dearborn's plan to attack Montreal ended in a botched attack on Lacolle Mills, between New York and Lower Canada (Quebec).

**Maj. Gen. Sir Isaac Brock, commander of British forces in Upper Canada, was killed at the Battle of Queenston Heights.**

### 1813: By Land and by Sea

Little changed in the new year. The British continued to defend their North American possessions and pursue a negotiated end to the war, while the Americans planned invasions along the Detroit and Niagara frontiers and another attempt on Montreal.

An advance American party along the Detroit frontier met defeat at the hands of British troops and their Native allies near Monroe, Michigan, in January 1813; the killing of U.S. prisoners by Britain's Native allies following the Battle of the River Raisin spawned a rallying cry to "Remember the River Raisin." After U.S. troops at Fort Meigs thwarted sieges in May and July, the British and their Native allies retreated to Detroit.

**The Niagara front** On April 27, American amphibious forces crossed Lake Ontario and captured York (now Toronto), the capital of Upper Canada (Ontario). They occupied York for a few days, captured cannon and other stores, burned government buildings, and returned to Sackets Harbor, New York.

In late May, U.S. forces destroyed Fort George with a massive artillery bombardment, followed by an amphibious invasion. The British, outnumbered four to one, retreated after a vicious battle. The American army occupied the town of Niagara and the ruins of Fort George as a bridgehead for the conquest of Upper Canada. However, defeats of U.S. armies at the Battle of Stoney Creek on June 6 and at Beaver Dams on June 24 forced the Americans back to Fort George, where the British and the Native allies besieged them for several months. The Americans abandoned Fort George on December 10, burning the Town of Niagara on their retreat. British troops advanced across the Niagara River, capturing Fort Niagara on December 19 and burning American settlements along the U.S. border.

**The Detroit front** Farther west, Captain Oliver Hazard Perry, commanding a small naval squadron constructed in Erie, Pennsylvania, met the British flotilla near Put-in-Bay. Perry forced the surrender of the British squadron at the Battle of Lake Erie on September 10, winning command of the lake and cutting off supplies to British military posts on the Detroit frontier. Forced to abandon Forts Detroit and Amherstburg, the retreating British and Native allies faced Harrison's army outside of Moraviantown. The victims of the U.S. victory at the ensuing Battle of the Thames included Tecumseh, killed by a bullet to the heart.

## The Montreal front

The American campaign against Montreal, the most ambitious of the war, involved two armies: One at Sackets Harbor, New York, under Maj. Gen. James Wilkinson, planned to sail down the St. Lawrence River while the other at Burlington, Vermont, under Maj. Gen. Wade Hampton, was to march north from Plattsburgh, New York, to meet Wilkinson at the St. Lawrence River west of Montreal. Neither army arrived: Canadian militia and Native allies turned back Hampton's army at the Battle of the Châteauguay on October 26, while the British defeated Wilkinson at the Battle of Crysler's Farm on November 11.

## The war at sea

Though American invasions of Canada were largely a failure, the small U.S. Navy scored several spectacular victories. With much of the British navy committed to a blockade of European ports, the small American fleet of a few powerful frigates proved its mettle. Two months after the outbreak of war, U.S.S. *Constitution* defeated the British frigate *Guerriere*. Additional U.S. victories in 1812 by the U.S.

## Key Dates 1813

✳ **JANUARY 18–23  BATTLE OF THE RIVER RAISIN (FRENCHTOWN)**

✳ **APRIL 27  U.S. ATTACKS AND CAPTURES YORK (TORONTO)**

✳ **MAY 1  BRITISH SIEGE OF FORT MEIGS**

✳ **MAY 27  U.S. CAPTURES FORT GEORGE**

✳ **MAY 27  BATTLE OF SACKETS HARBOR**

✳ **JUNE 1  H.M.S. *SHANNON* V. U.S.S. *CHESAPEAKE***

✳ **JUNE 6  BATTLE OF STONEY CREEK**

✳ **JUNE 22  BATTLE OF CRANEY ISLAND**

✳ **JUNE 24  BATTLE OF BEAVER DAMS**

✳ **AUGUST 30  BATTLE OF FORT MIMS**

✳ **SEPTEMBER 10  BATTLE OF LAKE ERIE**

✳ **OCTOBER 15  BATTLE OF THE THAMES**

✳ **OCTOBER 26  BATTLE OF THE CHÂTEAUGUAY**

✳ **NOVEMBER 11  BATTLE OF CRYSLER'S FARM**

✳ **DECEMBER 19  BRITISH CAPTURE FORT NIAGARA**

frigates *United States, Essex,* and *Constitution* raised American spirits. British naval morale plummeted until June 1, 1813, when H.M.S. *Shannon* captured the American frigate U.S.S. *Chesapeake* and sailed its prize to Halifax.

**Stalemate** At year's end, U.S. forces still occupied Canadian soil on the Detroit frontier but had failed to hold onto land captured in Niagara and could make no headway against Montreal. Time was running out: The U.S. government was bankrupt, the British blockade of American ports had devastated American businesses, and many citizens were lobbying for peace. There was even serious talk in New England of seceding from the union to make a separate peace with the British.

**The Creek War** The war involved Native Nations in the south as well as the north. In 1813, a civil war divided the Creek confederation of the Mississippi Territory, pitting Creeks who had chosen to accommodate aspects of white culture with others, known as Red Sticks, who opposed U.S. expansion into traditional Creek lands. A Red Sticks attack on Fort Mims, where a large number of Creek, Métis, and U.S. settlers had gathered for protection, transformed the civil war into a full-blown contest between the Red Sticks and U.S. militias. Andrew Jackson, at the command of a combined force of Tennessee militia and volunteers and Creek and Cherokee allies, defeated the Red Sticks at Horseshoe Bend on the Tallapoosa River on March 27, 1814, and then imposed land cessions on his Native foes and allies alike in the Treaty of Fort Jackson later that year.

## 1814: The Empire Strikes Back

With the defeat and abdication of Napoleon in March, Americans braced themselves for the redeployment of tens of thousands of seasoned British soldiers and hundreds of Royal Navy vessels. In Lower Canada (Quebec), the British stopped a U.S. advance on Montreal at Lacolle Mills near the New York border. On the Niagara frontier an American army scored a significant victory later that summer at the Battle of Chippawa following the surrender of Fort Erie to the Americans. After the Battle of Chippawa U.S. forces advanced on British fortifications at the mouth of the Niagara River, but were forced to retreat up the river when a

### Key Dates 1814

✻ **MARCH 27–28 BATTLE OF HORSESHOE BEND**

✻ **MARCH 28 H.M.S. *PHOEBE* AND H.M.S. *CHERUB* V. U.S.S. *ESSEX***

✻ **JULY 3 BATTLE OF FORT ERIE**

✻ **JULY 5 BATTLE OF CHIPPAWA**

✻ **JULY 25 BATTLE OF LUNDY'S LANE**

✻ **AUGUST 24 BATTLE OF BLADENSBURG**

✻ **SEPTEMBER 11 BATTLE OF PLATTSBURGH**

✻ **SEPTEMBER 12–14 BRITISH ATTACK BALTIMORE**

✻ **SEPTEMBER 13–14 BRITISH ATTACK FORT MCHENRY**

✻ **DECEMBER 14 BATTLE OF LAKE BORGNE**

✻ **DECEMBER 24 U.S. AND BRITAIN SIGN THE TREATY OF GHENT**

supporting U.S. naval squadron failed to arrive. Defeated at Lundy's Lane, the U.S. army retreated to Fort Erie, where they were besieged by the British. The British failed to recapture Fort Erie and suffered serious casualties in a direct assault on the U.S. defenses.

### The British offensive

The British devised an ambitious campaign aimed at forcing the Americans to negotiate a peace treaty while securing the borders of British North America from further U.S. attacks. Plans included the capture of Plattsburgh on Lake Champlain, attacks on Baltimore, a base for American privateers, and on the U.S. capital of Washington. They also planned to invade New Orleans. If successful, these attacks would force the Americans to accept British claims to the northern part of Maine while guaranteeing a sovereign Native territory west of the Ohio River. However, 1814 was remembered for U.S. victories on home soil.

Things started well for the British when, on August 15, they attacked Maryland and

**Andrew Jackson was a national hero after his victory over the British at the Battle of New Orleans and went on to become seventh President of the United States.**

routed U.S. militiamen at the Battle of Bladensburg, opening the road to Washington. British troops entered the capital and torched its public buildings, including the President's House, in retaliation for towns in Upper Canada burned by U.S. forces earlier in the war.

## Key Dates 1815

✳ **January 8** Battle of New Orleans

✳ **February 16** U.S. ratifies the Treaty of Ghent

✳ **June 30** U.S.S. *Peacock* defeats East India Cruiser *Nautilus*

**American victories** Elsewhere, success went to American arms. In September, a British force set out from Montreal to capture Plattsburgh, New York. While British soldiers occupied part of the town, their supporting naval flotilla was defeated in the Battle of Lake Champlain on September 11, forcing Lt. Gen. Sir George Prévost, the British commander in chief, to retreat.

A second British army planned an amphibious attack on Baltimore. British ships bombarded Fort McHenry for nearly 25 hours before abandoning the assault on September 14. Francis Scott Key immortalized Baltimore's stunning defense in song, penning a paean to the star-spangled banner that became the American national anthem.

The final thrust of Britain's 1814 campaign involved troops fresh from Europe arriving in the Gulf of Mexico. The Louisiana campaign began on December 13 and ended three weeks later at Chalmette Plantation, where Andrew Jackson and his army dealt this British force a crushing defeat at the Battle of New Orleans.

### 1815: Peace

Unknown to those fighting at New Orleans, an end to the war was negotiated in Belgium on Christmas Eve, 1814. On February 16, 1815, President James Madison signed the Treaty of Ghent and the War of 1812 was over. The treaty required both sides to return property captured during the war, called for a joint boundary commission to map the borders between the U.S. and British North America (later Canada), and confirmed prewar rights of Native Nations in lands controlled by the United States.

The treaty ushered in a lasting peace between the U.S. and its northern neighbor, and united British North Americans, who eventually joined their provinces into a confederation that remains a constitutional monarchy within the Commonwealth.

Present-day Map

Area Enlarged

CANADA

QUEBEC

Lake Superior

ONTARIO

Sault Ste. Marie

Fort St. Joseph NHS

Fort Mackinac (Mackinac Island State Park)

Ottawa

WISCONSIN

MICHIGAN

Lake Huron

Nancy Island Historic Site

Toronto

Lake Ontario

Madison

Lake Michigan

Milwaukee

NEW YORK

Chicago

Detroit

River Raisin National Battlefield Park

Fort Malden NHS

Lake Erie

Toledo

Fort Meigs State Memorial

Cleveland

Perry's Victory and International Peace Memorial

PENNSYLVANIA

Tippecanoe Battlefield Park

OHIO

Pittsburgh

ILLINOIS

UNITED    STATES

Columbus

Indianapolis

INDIANA

Cincinnati

WEST VIRGINIA

Washington, D.C.

VIRGINIA

George Rogers Clark NHP

St. Louis

Louisville

KENTUCKY

Present-day Map

■ National Historic Site (NHS)
■ National Historical Park (NHP)
□ Other
● Present-day major city

0          100 mi
0          100 km

# Old Northwest

The war in the Old Northwest (modern-day Ohio, Indiana, Illinois, Michigan, Wisconsin, and northeast Minnesota) was a microcosm of the conflict as a whole. For Americans, it was a chance to secure the western frontier and pursue territorial ambitions. The British hoped to defend their North American possessions. Members and factions within the Native Nations allied themselves with both sides in an effort to stave off European settlement in their ancestral homelands. Upper Canadians wanted to defend their land against American invasions and avoid annexation by the United States. Fought in the modern states of Ohio, Indiana, and Michigan, and in southern Ontario, the frontier war may have involved smaller forces than those in the eastern U.S., but the battles were fierce and featured Oliver Hazard Perry, William Henry Harrison, Sir Isaac Brock, and Tecumseh, some of the war's greatest leaders.

1

U.S. Commodore Oliver Hazard Perry, victor at the Battle of Lake Erie

## >> TIPPECANOE BATTLEFIELD PARK

One of the preludes to the War of 1812, the Battle of Tippecanoe took place in west-central Indiana in November 1811. In addition to being one of the sparks that ignited the war, the battle also propelled future President William Henry Harrison to national fame and, eventually, to the White House with the campaign slogan "Tippecanoe and Tyler Too."

When Harrison was appointed governor of the newly created Indiana Territory in 1800, one of his primary goals was to attract enough white settlers for it to qualify for statehood. In response, individuals from several Native Nations joined a confederation under the Shawnee prophet Tenskwatawa and his warrior-brother Tecumseh. When open hostilities ensued after the controversial 1809 Treaty of Fort Wayne, under which Harrison had negotiated the acquisition of 3 million acres (1.2 million ha) of Native Nations land for white settlers, Harrison marched an army of around 1,000 men against Prophetstown, Tecumseh's village of 20 to 30 lodges near the confluence of the Wabash and Tippecanoe Rivers.

Harrison hoped to destroy the stronghold while Tecumseh was away recruiting support. But confederation warriors struck first, attacking the American encampment on November 7. In two hours of fierce fighting, Harrison's troops took heavy casualties. With the coming of daylight the confederation warriors broke off the attack and abandoned Prophetstown. The Americans burned the village to the ground and destroyed any supplies they were not able to carry off.

The battle forced Tecumseh to relocate to Upper Canada and reorganize their

**A late 19th-century print of the Battle of Tippecanoe shows American troops repulsing a charge by Native warriors.**

resistance. Ultimately, it led to the very thing the Americans feared—a military alliance between Tecumseh's confederation and the British.

Today an 85-foot-high (26 m) **obelisk,** built in 1908 to commemorate the Tippecanoe centennial, marks the battlefield. An iron fence demarcates **Harrison's encampment.** Because many of the U.S. soldiers who died in the fighting were buried on the site, Americans regard the battlefield as a cemetery. The **museum** offers displays on the battle, the combatants, and the leaders on both sides. The weapons exhibit features more than 50 long guns, rifles, and other firearms dating from the War of 1812 and later.

200 Battle Ground Ave., Battle Ground, IN • 765-476-8411 • www.tippecanoe history.org • $ • Closed Wed.

## ❯❯ George Rogers Clark National Historical Park

Overlooking the Wabash River in Vincennes, George Rogers Clark National Historical Park pays tribute to the older brother of explorer William Clark (of Lewis and Clark fame). Instrumental in bringing the Old Northwest Territory into the fledgling United States, George was one of the unsung heroes of the American Revolution. But this remote corner was also the scene of critical events—such as

### Quick History

While neither side was victorious on the battlefield, the burning of Prophetstown by Harrison's troops was seen as a major step in reducing the threat of ongoing war in the Old Northwest. Tecumseh had no choice but to ally himself with the British in Upper Canada once the War of 1812 broke out. And Native resistance to white settlement of the Wabash Valley continued after the battle. That did not prevent Harrison reminding voters of his victory during his two presidential runs three decades later, including at a massive rally at the battlefield in 1840 attended by an estimated 30,000 people.

the 1811 Tippecanoe Campaign—that helped to shape the War of 1812.

The imposing **Clark Memorial** at the heart of the park in Vincennes sits on the site of Fort Sackville—a British bastion captured by Clark during the Revolution. The circular granite memorial features 16 Doric columns and a glass-roofed rotunda overlooking the Wabash River. Inside are a statue of Clark by Hermon Atkins MacNeil and murals by Ezra Winter depicting Clark's 1778 Ohio Valley campaign.

In 1787, the Americans constructed a new fort, Fort Knox I on the site of Fort Sackville, but because of tensions between the town and the garrison, in 1803 they built another fort, **Fort Knox II,** about 3 miles (5 km) north of Vincennes. Harrison used Fort Knox II as the jumping-off point for his campaign in the Wabash Valley that culminated in the Battle of Tippecanoe. In 1813, U.S. commanders decided that Fort Knox II's location a few miles outside town left it vulnerable to attack. They had it dismantled, floated down the Wabash, and rebuilt near the site of Fort Knox I. Partially reconstructed wooden palisades and interpretive signs mark out the original site of Fort Knox II today.

401 S. 2nd St., Vincennes, IN • 812-882-1776 • www.nps.gov/gero

## » FORT MACKINAC
## MACKINAC ISLAND STATE PARK

**Built by the British during the American Revolution to control the strategic straits between upper and lower Michigan, Fort Mackinac played a pivotal role in control of the Great Lakes during the War of 1812. The two sides squared off twice here (in 1812 and 1814), both battles ending in British victory, but the Treaty of Ghent at the end of the war returned the region to the Americans.**

Overlooking Lake Huron's Haldimand Bay on the south side of Mackinac Island, the limestone-and-timber fort perches on a bluff with a commanding view of the Straits of Mackinac. Constructed in the early 1780s, it passed into American control in 1796 under the terms of Jay's Treaty.

Despite its isolation, the fort was an immediate focus of British interest when hostilities between America and Britain broke out again in 1812. The initial clash over Mackinac took place on July 17, when Capt. Charles Roberts, the British garrison commander at Fort St. Joseph (see pp. 24–26), made the first strike. The captain complemented his force of 40 British regulars with 150 fur-trade employees and around 300 Native allies. They crossed the 45 miles (72 km) between St. Joseph and Mackinac Island in a flotilla composed of a schooner, Northwest Company (a fur-trading company) bateaux, and freighter canoes. After evacuating civilians from the village and wheeling a field gun into place to bombard Fort Mackinac, Roberts was ready to attack. But it never got that far. The fort was so isolated and frontier communication so poor that U.S. commander Porter Hanks was not aware that war had been declared and

was ill-prepared to defend against a British assault. Assuming that he was outgunned and overmatched, Hanks decided that surrender was the better course of action.

Two years later, the Americans were back in force as part of a campaign to retake the upper Great Lakes. On July 26, 1814, five American warships and 700 troops under the command of Lt. Col. George Croghan arrived off the island. American naval guns attempted to pound the fort for a couple of days, but could not be raised to a high enough elevation. On August 4, rowboats ferried American troops to the north shore to start what Croghan assumed was a surprise attack. But the British were waiting in the woods. The garrison of 140 soldiers of the Royal Newfoundland Regiment and 150 Menominee allies drove off the American force of 700 men. The fort remained in British hands until the end of the war.

## Nearby & Noteworthy

✴ **AMERICAN FUR COMPANY WAREHOUSE** The company used this L-shaped edifice built in 1810 for processing beaver, mink, muskrat, and other pelts before shipment to eastern markets. *Market at Astor St., Mackinac Island Village, MI, www.mackinac.com*

✴ **WAWASHKAMO GOLF CLUB** The 1814 Battle of Mackinac played out on what is now the Wawashkamo golf course. Some of the 200-year-old red oaks are "battle trees" that bore witness to the fighting. *3723 British Landing Rd., Mackinac Island, MI, www.wawashkamo.com*

**Fort remains** Today, the buildings of Fort Mackinac are the oldest in Michigan and an integral part of Mackinac State Historic Parks, six units that preserve heritage sites around the island. Among the 14 original structures are the post headquarters, hospital, guardhouse, bathhouse, and various barracks. Three **blockhouses** (built in 1798), the **Wood Quarters** (1816), and the **Officers' Stone Quarters** (1780) where the post commanders and their families lived, date from around the time of the War of 1812. Inside are period furnishings and interactive displays on the fort's history, family life, and military training.

Living history events take place during the season, including a vintage baseball game played using 19th-century rules and no gloves. Another popular event involves the cleaning, loading, and firing of an 1841 6-pound, smoothbore field gun over the bay. Music from bygone times, dancing, military drills, and children's games are also part of the living history experience. ∎

7127 Huron Rd., Mackinac Island, MI • 906-847-3328 • www.mackinacparks.com/fort-mackinac • $ • Closed early Oct. to early May

The gun platform on Fort Mackinac's south side offers superb views of the town and the Straits of Mackinac.

# » Fort St. Joseph National Historic Site

When the British handed over Fort Mackinac to the Americans in 1796, they decided to create a new military post to protect their interests in the upper Great Lakes and solidify their alliances with the Native Nations in the region. They chose a strategically placed peninsula on nearby St. Joseph Island, Ontario, and garrisoned the fort with a small detachment of troops. During its short existence, Fort St. Joseph was a military post and thriving fur-trade center.

Situated at the meeting point of three of the Great Lakes (Superior, Huron, and Michigan), Fort St. Joseph's primary purposes were to protect and foster the lucrative fur trade that passed through the region and to anchor British claims to all territory north of St. Marys River. As such, it attracted a small population of Northwest Company employees, who established a community outside the fort. With a British Indian Department agent stationed there, the settlement also saw a steady flow of Anishinaabeg visitors. As the most westerly outpost of British North America, Fort St. Joseph was lonely, remote, and largely cut off from communication with the rest of Canada.

When war broke out in the summer of 1812, the isolated and weakly fortified post was suddenly thrust to the forefront of international geopolitics. Rather than wait for an assault that his troops might not be able to repel, garrison commander Capt. Charles Roberts, who had received

orders from his superior, Maj. Gen. Sir Isaac Brock, to take the initiative, devised a plan to hit the Americans first by capturing Fort Mackinac, which he did with a swift and

**Ongoing archaeological excavations at Fort St. Joseph have revealed the outlines and remains of a number of buildings, including the blockhouse and kitchens.**

secret attack (see p. 22). His combined force of British regulars, fur-trade employees, and Native allies surprised the American garrison, who had not yet received news of the outbreak of war. Outnumbered and isolated, the American commander surrendered without a shot being fired.

**The British relocate** Having thwarted the only American threat in the region, Roberts relocated his command from St. Joseph's to Mackinac, a much more substantial fort on a piece of land that would be easier to defend if U.S. forces counterattacked. The fur traders went too, moving their operations to Mackinac village. Fort St. Joseph, barely

15 years old, stood empty. Although abandoned, it was not completely forgotten, because in the summer of 1814, an American naval force under Col. George Croghan cruised up St. Marys River with the aim of capturing Fort St. Joseph as the first step in a campaign to retake control of the upper Great Lakes (see pp. 22–23). Much to their surprise, the fort was vacant. But that did not prevent them from torching the buildings before sailing on to defeat at Mackinac.

Although they were forced to return Fort Mackinac to the Americans after the war and move back to their side of the border, the British decided not to rebuild Fort St. Joseph. Instead, they developed

a new base on nearby Drummond Island (see box below), which at the time was considered to be in British North American territory. A survey after the war determined that it was in the U.S.

**The past revealed** Weeds soon ruled the ruins of Fort Joseph, which faded into history until the 1920s, when the Sault Ste. Marie (Ontario) Historical Society decided to preserve this small chapter of Canadian history. The site had gone virtually untouched for more than a hundred years and had escaped looting by souvenir hunters, making it a prime candidate for

preservation. Archaeological digs have uncovered the remains of more than 40 structures on the tiny peninsula.

A small **museum** in the fort's visitor center tells the story of Fort St. Joseph and of the commercial and cultural relationship between Europeans and Native Nations in this remote corner of Ontario. Visitors can watch films about the fur trade and the archaeological digs, and see artifacts uncovered at the site. Other exhibits include uniforms and clothing worn by soldiers and the Anishinaabeg and other nations who frequented the fort.

From the visitor center, footpaths spread out across the peninsula to the ruins, most prominent of which is the old **blockhouse,** a rectangle of stones in the middle of a field not far from the lakeshore. Nearby are the remains of the **powder magazine,** a **guard house,** and a couple of **kitchens,** whose chimneys are the most recognizable features today. Those with keen eyesight may be able to identify the outline of the fort walls and the triangular bastions at the four corners.

Visitors can also wander nature trails. People have spotted black bear, moose, beaver, and eagles in and around the historic site. Wildlife also flourishes in the **St. Joseph's Island Migratory Bird Sanctuary** around the fort.

Those with an interest in living history should visit Fort St. Joseph in mid-August, when volunteers present the annual **Ghost Walk,** an after-dark candlelight stroll through the ruins. "Spirits" in period costumes recount tales of what life was like during the early 19th century. ∎

**Fort Rd., St. Joseph Island, ON • 705-246-2664 • www.parkscanada.ca • $ • Closed mid-Oct. to June**

## Nearby & Noteworthy

✴ **FORT DRUMMOND** Ruins are all that remain of the base the British built in 1815 to replace Fort Mackinac—without realizing that it was on U.S. territory. The ruins are now on private property and visitors can view them only from the water. A historical marker just east of the Drummond Island ferry dock describes the fort. *Drummond Island, MI, www.drummond islandchamber.com*

✴ **ST. JOSEPH ISLAND MUSEUM** Located near the island's north end, the museum's 6,000-plus collection includes Fort St. Joseph relics and Native Nations artifacts. Historic structures, such as the first schoolhouse, a general store, and the old Zion Church, have been moved to the museum village. *20th Side Rd. and 1 Line, St. Joseph Island, ON, www.stjoemuseum.com*

✴ **SAULT STE. MARIE** A fur-trading center in the war, this Michigan city boasts a number of structures dating from that time. The Sault Tribe of Chippewa Indians Interpretive Center describes the history and customs of the region's primary Native Nations group. *523 Ashmun St., Sault Ste. Marie, MI, www.saultstemarie.com*

## » *Fort Malden (Amherstburg) National Historic Site*

**Built on the Canadian side of the Detroit River near its confluence with Lake Erie, Fort Malden commands one of the most strategic points in the Great Lakes. At the outbreak of war, the site was home to the British naval base for Lake Erie. Within a month it came under attack from the Americans, and throughout the war it changed hands between British and U.S. forces. The current layout is largely attributed to the Americans, who occupied the base for the better part of two years.**

In the negotiations that resulted in Jay's Treaty (1796), the British agreed to turn Detroit over to the U.S. They scouted for a nearby location that would fill the strategic gap and assume the dual roles of protecting British economic interests in the region and

managing relations with the Native Nations. They chose a waterfront site on what is now the north side of Amherstburg, Ontario, and began developing a combined naval and army base.

The shipyard included a dock, workshops, rope-making facility, and barracks for a company of Provincial Marines. Nearby rose a complex of buildings enclosed within a square palisaded earthwork fortification

**"View of Amherstburg," painted in 1813 by Margaret Reynolds, shows the yard where the British navy constructed ships.**

with bastions or artillery positions protecting each corner of the fort. The complex included a blockhouse, barracks, and a council house where the British Indian Department conducted affairs with Native Nations visitors.

Barely a month into the war, an American force crossed the Detroit River and approached Amherstburg from the north. But the British beat them back in the Battle of the River Canard on July 16, a skirmish that produced the war's first British casualty. Shortly afterward British commander Maj. Gen. Sir Isaac Brock and the Shawnee leader Tecumseh—who had traveled to Upper Canada to seek an alliance with the British after the Battle of Tippecanoe (see pp. 20–21)—met at Fort Amherstburg to plan the attack that captured Detroit in August (see box right).

**U.S. blockade** The British hoped to use Amherstburg to launch raids on northern Ohio and other American territory, but they knew that they did not have control of Lake Erie as long as there were American vessels on the lake. And they had not reckoned with American tenacity and maritime expertise. By the summer of 1813, the Americans had enough warships on the lake to threaten British supply lines to the Detroit frontier. British naval Cmdr. Robert Barclay intended to end the blockade by destroying the American fleet. Instead, it was the British squadron that surrendered at the end of the fateful Battle of Lake Erie on September 10 (see pp. 32–33).

**Battle of the Thames** With the British Lake Erie squadron captured and the Americans in control of the lake, there was no way that supplies could reach Amherstburg. After torching the fort and naval yard, the British persuaded reluctant Native allies to retreat inland. The Americans under Gen. William Henry Harrison pursued them, catching up in early October. The ensuing Battle of the Thames, near present-day Chatham, Ontario, resulted in a decisive U.S. victory and the death of Tecumseh, without whose leadership the Confederacy lost its sense of unity.

The Americans occupied the site at Amherstburg for the remainder of the war, building a new, smaller fort and erecting a few modest structures. By 1815, the conflict was over and the base was once again in British hands. They rebuilt the fort on the site of the first one and named it Fort Malden. With ongoing peace between Britain and the United States, the fort became less important as a strategic asset and was demilitarized in 1858. For

## Quick History

The Siege of Detroit by the British in summer 1812 followed two months of skirmishing along the Detroit River corridor. Before marching on the American stronghold, General Brock sent a dispatch to U.S. commander William Hull demanding surrender and hinting at a massacre by his Native allies if battle should ensue. Brock also rattled Hull with ingenious bluffs (such as multiple campfires) that made his force seem larger than it was. A British bombardment from the Canadian shore further softened American resolve. Assuming he was greatly outnumbered, Hull surrendered on August 16, 1812.

A reenactor at Fort Malden gives a demonstration of blacksmithing, one of the essential skills of fort life.

a short time, it served as a branch of the Provincial Lunatic Asylum.

**Living history** Decked out in the uniform of the war-era Caldwell's Western Rangers or the 34th Regiment of Foot from the Canadian Rebellions (insurrections against British rule in 1837 and 1838), Parks Canada personnel lead living history programs and interpretive tours. Most of the buildings date from its reconstruction after the War of 1812 or its decade as an asylum.

Located in a building constructed for the lunatic asylum, the **interpretive center museum** boasts one of Canada's finest War of 1812 collections, including uniforms, weapons, and period furnishings. Among its most prized relics are two sets of wampum strings that once belonged to Tecumseh, U.S. Gen. James Winchester's pistols and

sword surrendered at the Battle of the River Raisin (see pp. 34–35), and Margaret Reynolds' "View of Amherstburg" (see p. 27).

Fort Malden also organizes educational programs and special events, including Military Heritage Days in August when tactical demonstrations, military encampments, and children's activities related to military history through the ages fill the grounds. Guided tours start from the Visitor Orientation Centre and cover fort architecture, early 19th-century living conditions, and the importance of Amherstburg as a British military and naval base. ■

**100 Laird Ave., Amherstburg, ON • 519-736-5416 • www.parkscanada.ca • $**

## ≫ Fort Meigs State Memorial

**The British followed up their victory at the River Raisin in January 1813 by invading northern Ohio in the spring of 1813. To hold onto Detroit and Michigan territory, they needed to destroy the American naval facilities at Presque Isle on Lake Erie. But they could not attack Presque Isle by land and leave Fort Meigs, an American outpost in what is now suburban Toledo, Ohio, to threaten their line of march.**

When Gen. William Henry Harrison established Fort Meigs in early 1813 as a supply depot and staging ground for the American campaign to retake Detroit and the upper Great Lakes, he never intended it to be a permanent base. But when the campaign stalled after the crushing American defeat at the River Raisin (see pp. 34–35), the riverside encampment developed into a proper fort guarding the land route to and from Canada.

During the spring and summer of 1813, British and Canadian forces, along with Native allies, twice laid siege to Fort Meigs. Both times they failed and were forced to retreat back to Canada. After the American victory at the Battle of Lake Erie (see pp. 32–33) in September 1813 and subsequent invasion of southern Ontario, General Harrison had Fort Meigs dismantled because the garrison he had left behind was too small to adequately defend an installation of that size. Instead, he ordered that a smaller fortification be built, including a small wooden stockade, that could be defended by a smaller garrison. American forces abandoned the fort in 1815 and soon afterward it burned to the ground.

A 100-foot-tall (30 m) **monument** erected in 1908 commemorates the fort's role in the War of 1812. Then, during the late 1960s, the Ohio Historical Society reconstructed the fort using descriptions from journals, diaries, military manuals, and other sources. The stockade was rebuilt in 2001–2003.

**The reconstructed fort** Comprising more than 3,000 individual logs, called "pickets," sunk 3 feet (0.9 m) into the ground and 15 feet (4.5 m) tall, the reconstructed fort is the largest log fort in the United States. The

10-acre (4 ha) enclosure includes seven wooden blockhouses, five artillery emplacements, and a quartermaster's warehouse, as well as the 1908 granite obelisk. Interactive exhibits inside the blockhouses tell of how the fort was built, what life was like for the soldiers who manned it, and what transpired during the two sieges.

The **visitor center** near the main gate explains Ohio's role in the War of 1812 through modern exhibits that revolve around the themes of era, conflict, understanding, and remembrance. From weapons and munitions to kitchenware and uniform parts, nearly 90 percent of the Ohio Historical Society's War of 1812 **artifact collection** is on display at Fort Meigs. One of the most precious items is the intricately decorated powder horn made by Francis

### Quick History

Running short on munitions during the first siege of Fort Meigs, legend holds that General Harrison offered a reward of 1 gill of whiskey to any soldier who retrieved British cannonballs fired at the fort. Nearly 400 were handed in to the fort's quartermaster. The garrison added to its rations by fishing in the adjacent Maumee River. Even today, the river is known for its walleye and white bass angling.

Tansel, a volunteer with Boswell's 10th Kentucky Militia stationed at the fort. A video tells the story of Fort Meigs and the twin sieges.

Living history programs are central to the visitor experience. Of particular note are the annual First Siege Reenactment, in May; the Memorial Day Commemoration; and July 4 celebrations, when the fort bustles with mock battles, musket and cannon demonstrations, and meticulously replicated camps on the fort's grassy parade grounds. ■

**29100 West River Rd., Perrysburg, OH • 800-283-8916 • www.fortmeigs.org • $ • Closed Mon. and Tues.; fort closed Oct. to April**

The reconstruction of Fort Meigs is based on the appearance of the original fort during the two sieges of 1813.

## »Perry's Victory and International Peace Memorial

On September 10, 1813, British and American naval squadrons clashed in a three-hour battle on Lake Erie that ended with the capture by the Americans of the entire British squadron on the lake. Two hundred years later, a 352-foot-tall (107 m) column overlooking the battle site in the waters off northern Ohio commemorates the bloody encounter—the greatest naval battle of the war—and the long-lasting peace that followed between the U.S., Britain, and Canada.

The maritime battle on Lake Erie was the culmination of a yearlong struggle for control of the lake and its strategic shipping lanes. The British navy had the upper hand at first, but in spring 1813 U.S. Captain Oliver Hazard Perry was put in charge of expanding the U.S. fleet there. With the completion of several new ships and the addition of other vessels towed up the Niagara River from Lake Ontario, Perry's fleet grew in strength to the point where it menaced British supply routes to Amherstburg (see p. 28). With the garrison starving, the British had no choice but to surprise and destroy Perry's fleet.

**Battle of Lake Erie** At dawn, British Cmdr. Robert Barclay—a veteran of the Battle of Trafalgar during the Napoleonic Wars in Europe—led a squadron of six warships across the lake and into American waters. After a lookout on Rattlesnake Island spotted the British approaching, Perry mobilized nine American ships. Sailing out of Put-in-Bay harbor, his force engaged the British for more than three hours.

Although outgunned and with fewer experienced seamen, the British had the upper hand at the beginning of the battle. Then, with his flagship U.S. Brig *Lawrence* badly damaged and the British on the verge of victory, Perry opted for one of the riskiest moves in U.S. naval history—piloting a rowboat through the middle of the fray to the undamaged U.S. Brig *Niagara*. With fresh canvas overhead and a battery of 20 guns, Perry sailed through the heart of the British fleet. Firing from both sides, *Niagara* devastated the enemy ships, forcing the wounded Barclay to surrender.

**Perry's Victory Memorial on South Bass Island overlooks Put-in-Bay. An elevator whisks visitors to an open-air observation deck 317 feet (97 m) above the ground.**

### Quick History

Born in 1785, the son of a Rhode Island naval captain, Oliver Hazard Perry decided that seafaring was his destiny too. As a midshipman, he served on many celebrated American ships (including U.S.S. *Constitution*) and sailed the Barbary Coast, as well as sailing to Europe and Africa. By age 23, he had his own command, a 14-gun schooner, U.S.S. *Revenge.* When war broke out in 1812, Perry was promoted to master-commandant and in 1813 he was given a command on Lake Erie, where the Americans were building a fleet to challenge British control of the lake. In 1819, Perry was sent on a diplomatic mission to Venezuela. On the return journey he contracted yellow fever, and died near Trinidad on August 23, 1819—his 34th birthday.

The British suffered 41 killed to 27 on the American side. Perry penned the phrase "We have met the enemy and they are ours" in a letter to Gen. William Henry Harrison proclaiming the American victory.

**Battle memorial** Erected between 1912 and 1915 to honor the battle centennial, the **Victory Monument** on South Bass Island is the world's largest Doric column (47 feet / 14 m taller than the Statue of Liberty). Etched into the rotunda walls are the names of the nine U.S. warships that took part in the battle and of every American who was killed or wounded in the battle. Beneath the rotunda floor are the bodies of three American and three British officers who died during the battle.

A **visitor center** on Toledo Avenue offers displays, talks, and an audio-visual presentation on the Battle of Lake Erie and the War of 1812. On summer weekends, rangers dressed in War of 1812 uniforms and civilian garb give talks on the battle and the war and give musket and cannon-firing demonstrations. ∎

93 Delaware Ave., Put-in-Bay, OH • 419-285-2184 • www.nps.gov/pevi • $ • Visitor Center closed late Oct. to mid-April; observation deck closed late Oct. to early July

# »River Raisin National Battlefield Park

**"Remember the Raisin" became an American rallying cry of the War of 1812. Coined after the killing of American prisoners following the Battle of the River Raisin in southern Michigan in early 1813, the catchphrase helped muster civilians behind the war effort and rouse U.S. troops to retake the Old Northwest frontier.**

The Battle of the River Raisin (also known as the Battle of Frenchtown) consisted of a series of attacks and counterattacks that played out between January 18 and 23, 1813, around Frenchtown, a small community at the western end of Lake Erie. Captured by British and Native forces early in the war, the town lay in the path of an American army trying to retake Detroit and control of the upper Great Lakes. Acting without orders from the high command, an American force under Gen. James Winchester advanced on the town. Although it comprised mostly untrained Kentuckians and local French militia, the group flushed the British from Frenchtown on January 18.

British forces lingered in the area and were soon reinforced by regular troops and artillery from Amherstburg and more than 800 Native warriors, mostly Potawatomi. Meanwhile, an overconfident Winchester ignored warnings from local residents that the enemy was nearby and failed to secure the town. Early on January 22, the British and their allies attacked. After several hours of heavy fighting and considerable casualties, Winchester surrendered. Nearly

**Modern-day members of Lacroix's Michigan militia take part in the annual tribute to the Battle of the River Raisin, which remembers the Americans, French, British, Canadians, and Native warriors who fought in it.**

300 Americans were killed on that day—likely the greatest single-day loss of life for U.S. forces during the war. The British captured more than 500 U.S. troops, and the British commander pledged to protect American prisoners from Native retribution.

**The aftermath** If the bloodshed had ended there, River Raisin would have been just another battle in the three-year conflict. But over the next 24 hours, one of the most controversial episodes of the war took place. The British regulars departed Frenchtown, marching most of the prisoners back to Amherstburg. Those not able to walk were left behind to recuperate under the care of several American surgeons and British

A pistol belonging to General Winchester, commander of U.S. forces at the Battle of River Raisin

interpreters. On the morning of January 23, Native warriors allied with the British killed dozens of wounded prisoners before leaving town—an incident that was dubbed the "River Raisin Massacre" by enraged Americans.

As a result of the battle, Winchester's army was decimated. Harrison was forced to cancel his winter campaign to retake Detroit, and the Americans would take more than six months to recover their military strength in the Great Lakes theater.

**Battle memorial**
Frenchtown endured the war, but in 1817 changed its name to Monroe in honor of then-President James Monroe. Although memorialized by locals as the bloodiest battle on Michigan soil and remembered in Kentucky because that state bore the bulk of the U.S. casualties,

River Raisin was not honored nationally until 1982, when the battlefield was added to the National Register of Historic Places. It became a national battlefield park in 2009, one of the newest units of the National Park Service.

Centerpiece of the park is a **visitor center** with multimedia exhibits and displays of wartime weapons, uniforms, and other artifacts. A fiber-optic map presentation tells the story of River Raisin and the Great Lakes campaign. Elsewhere are full-scale vignettes of participants and dioramas of the landmark battles of the River Raisin, Lake Erie, and the Thames. Trails lead to **monuments,** vintage **artillery pieces,** and plaques around the battlefield. ∎

1403 East Elm Ave., Monroe, MI • 734-243-7136 • www.nps.gov/rira

## Nearby & Noteworthy

✳ **EPIDEMIC MONUMENT** More than 700 U.S. prisoners held in Detroit perished in the winter of 1813–1814 from a cholera-like epidemic and were buried in a mass grave. A historic marker recalls the incident. *Washington Blvd. and Michigan Ave., Detroit, MI, www.visitdetroit.com*

✳ **KENTUCKY MONUMENT** Erected in 1904, this monument honors the Kentucky militiamen who died at River Raisin during the battle and in the killing of prisoners. *West 7th and South Monroe Sts., Monroe, MI, www.historicmonroe.org*

✳ **MONGUAGON BATTLEFIELD** On August 9, 1812, 600 U.S. troops defeated a force of British troops and Native allies at Monguagon. A marker in Elizabeth Park commemorates the battle. *3873 West Jefferson, Trenton, MI, www.waymarking.com*

✳ **NAVARRE-ANDERSON TRADING POST** Erected in 1789, this clapboard structure is one of the oldest wooden residences in Michigan. During the war it served as a military hospital. *3775 North Custer Rd., Monroe, MI, www.historic monroe.org*

## ❯❯ *Nancy Island Historic Site*

Made from oak and red cedar, an 80-foot (24 m) lake schooner called the *Nancy* was launched in Detroit in 1789. For more than two decades, it served the upper Great Lakes fur trade, but when war broke out in 1812 the British requisitioned the boat and transformed it into an armed transportation vessel. During the Battle of Lake Erie (see pp. 32–33), the *Nancy* was on a mission to Mackinac Island and avoided the fate of the rest of the British fleet.

As the only remaining Royal Navy ship on the Upper Lakes, the *Nancy* ran supplies between isolated British outposts. During a voyage in summer 1814, its skipper, Lt. Miller Worsley, learned that American ships were roaming Lake Huron in search of British targets. Worsley slipped the *Nancy* 2 miles (3 km) up the Nottawasaga River and built a blockhouse on the adjacent shore to protect it in case of enemy attack.

On August 14, sailors gathering wood for three U.S. warships discovered the *Nancy*. The Americans opened fire, badly damaging the schooner. Worsley ordered the boat to be burned to prevent it falling into American hands. Then he and his men escaped inland and paddled 360 miles (580 km) to the British base on Mackinac Island.

Over the ensuing years, the sunken ship created a natural dam on the Nottawasaga, eventually trapping enough silt to form an island. Rediscovered in 1911 and raised onto the island in 1928, the **hull** now forms the centerpiece of an interpretive center dedicated to H.M.S. *Nancy* and its crew. Housed beneath an avant-garde roof inspired by the sight of sails straining against the Great Lakes wind, the museum features a short film about the ship and displays of War of 1812 artifacts.

**119 Mosely St., Wasaga Beach, ON • 705-429-2516 • www.wasagabeachpark.com • $ • Closed early Sept. to late June**

Nancy Island hosts "Wasaga Under Siege," an annual living history festival each August.

## >> OTHER SITES & PLAQUES

### ♣ AMHERSTBURG NAVY YARD

The Amherstburg Navy Yard National Historic Site in southwest Ontario marks the spot where British forces built most of their Great Lakes fleet during the War of 1812. **270 Dalhousie St., Amherstburg, ON • 519-736-0012 • www.amherstburg.ca**

### ♣ BATTLE OF THE LONGWOODS

A cairn and descriptive plaque at the Battle Hill National Historic Site near Wardsville marks the site of the battle on March 4, 1814, which pitted U.S. troops against British regulars, Canadian militia, Potawatomis, and Wyandots. **2945 Longwoods Rd., Wardsville, ON • www.royal-scots.com**

### ♣ BATTLE OF MALCOLM'S MILLS

A historical plaque marks the site of a short but fierce battle waged on November 6, 1814, during which an American force of 700 men under Gen. Duncan McArthur overwhelmed 150 Canadian militiamen. **Pioneer Cemetery, Rd. 24, Oakland, ON**

### ★ ERIE MARITIME MUSEUM

The museum recalls the Battle of Lake Erie with displays, interpretive programs, and a reconstruction of U.S.S. *Niagara*, Oliver Hazard Perry's second flagship during the battle. **150 East Front St., Erie, PA • 814-452-2744 • www.eriemaritimemuseum.org**

### ♣ HER MAJESTY'S ROYAL CHAPEL OF THE MOHAWKS

The chapel was built for the Mohawk village at Brant's Ford to replace one built by Queen Anne in the Mohawk valley that was lost to the Americans in the Revolutionary War. Mohawk warriors fought with the British in several battles in the War of 1812. **301 Mohawk St., Brantford, ON • 519-756-0240 • www.mohawkchapel.ca**

### ★ MISSISSINEWA BATTLEFIELD

The Battle of Mississinewa, during which U.S. forces destroyed four Miami Native villages, took place on December 17–18, 1812, near present-day Marion, IN. Three markers and an annual reenactment recall the battle's cost. **County Rd. 360W near County Rd. West 600N, La Fontaine, IN • 800-822-1812 • www.mississinewa1812.com**

### ★ PRESQUE ISLE NAVAL BASE

Presque Isle was the home port of the American fleet that won the Battle of Lake Erie in September 1813. The Perry Monument at Crystal Point in Presque Isle State Park commemorates the American victory and sailors who fell in the battle. **301 Peninsula Dr., Erie, PA • 814-833-7424 • www.dcnr.state.pa.us**

### ★ PROPHETSTOWN

Prophetstown State Park and the Historic Prophetstown Museum offer pioneer-era buildings, a reproduction woodland Indian settlement, and restored prairie-woodland habitat on the site of Tecumseh's capital. **5545 Swisher Rd., West Lafayette, IN • 765-567-4919 or 765-567-4700 • www.prophetstown.org**

### ♣ TECUMSEH (BATTLE OF THE THAMES) MONUMENT

Shawnee leader Tecumseh fought alongside the British and was killed at the Battle of the Thames. He is honored by a roadside memorial near modern-day Thamesville, Ontario. **14421 Longwoods Rd., Thamesville, ON**

2

Oshawa

Toronto

Lake Ontario

Hamilton

Old Fort Niagara
State Historic Site
Fort Mississauga NHS
Fort George NHS
Queenston Heights NHS;
The Colored Corps;
Vrooman's Battery NHS
Lewiston

Battle of
Stoney Creek
NHS

ONTARIO

C A N A D A

Battle of Beaver Dams NHS
Lundy's Lane NHS
Battle of Chippawa NHS

Niagara Falls

Battle of Cooks Mills

Grand

Fort Erie NHS
Buffalo

NEW YORK

Lake Erie

UNITED STATES

Chautauqua
Lake

National Historic Site (NHS)
Other
Present-day major city

0                    20 mi

0                    20 km

Present-day Map

Presque
Isle

Erie Maritime
Museum

Erie

Jamestown

PENNSYLVANIA

Area
Enlarged

Present-day Map

# NIAGARA REGION

In the Niagara region warring nations sat side by side, separated by only the narrow ribbon of the Niagara River and its powerful falls. Control of the river was vital to both Britain and the U.S., since it was the main transportation corridor between Lake Ontario and Lake Erie. The region also formed part of the homelands of the Haudenosaunee (Six Nations), which allied themselves with either the British or American cause. Fort George, the headquarters of the British army and the British Indian Department in Upper Canada, presided over the left bank of the river's mouth, in clear view of America's Fort Niagara opposite. Farther south, Fort Schlosser stood on the American border, while Fort Chippawa and Fort Erie were strategic points near the entrance to Lake Erie. Today, a journey along the banks of the river and into the interior on both sides of the border takes in many of the major battle sites as well as fascinating points in between.

A Canadian powder horn, used in the 1813 Battle of Beaver Dams

# »Fort George National Historic Site

**The war had been raging for almost a year when, on May 25, 1813, U.S. forces fired red-hot cannonballs on Fort George. Guarding the Niagara River, the link between Lake Ontario and the Great Lakes to the west, the fort had been primed for an attack from early in the war. Several hundred British regulars defended the fort, along with Canadian militia and Native allies, but they were heavily outnumbered by the American troops who advanced along the river in May.**

After vacating Fort Niagara, in Youngstown, New York, under the terms of Jay's Treaty of 1794, the British built a new fortification on the other side of the Niagara River, near the Town of Niagara, now Niagara-on-the-Lake (Ontario). They completed Fort George in 1802.

When war broke out in 1812, the Americans hoped to use Niagara as a foothold for their expansion into Upper Canada, and the fort became a key target for a U.S. assault. This failed to happen during the first year of the war. Artillerymen on both sides of the river fired at each other from time to time but caused little damage.

The U.S. bombardment on May 25, 1813, destroyed much of the large wooden fortress. Brig. Gen. John Vincent and his small garrison had little time to prepare for the next American offensive, which came two days later. On May 27, more than a dozen ships carried 5,000 U.S. troops to the landing 2 miles (3 km) from Fort George. The British came out to meet the offensive but, outnumbered five to one, were pushed back. Forced to abandon the fort, they retreated to Burlington Heights.

The Town of Niagara and the fort fell to American forces, but after U.S. defeats at Stoney Creek and Beaver Dams the Americans abandoned Fort George on December 10, 1813, burning the fort and the Town of Niagara in their wake. Immediately afterward the British reoccupied the fort, partially rebuilding it

## Quick History

Cannon, made of iron or bronze, were vital to all the armies fighting in the War of 1812. Some cannon were mobile and could be wheeled around during battle, while others were placed in fixed places such as forts. Whatever their size, their operation was similar. Ammunition (cannonballs) and gunpowder were loaded into the cannon through the muzzle, at the front. The powder was then ignited, forcing the ammunition out. The size of a cannon was measured by the weight of the cannonballs it could fire, with the most common of the large guns firing 24-pound (10 kg) balls.

in 1814. However, the newly constructed Fort Mississauga (see p. 56), a mile (2 km) north of Fort George, on the mouth of the Niagara River, was farther from the American shore and more secure. By the 1830s Fort George was in ruins.

**The battlefield and fort** Less than two miles (3 km) from Fort George, at the northwest end of Queen Street, Niagara-on-the Lake, a stone cairn with a bronze plaque marks the northeast corner of the **battlefield,** but the main portion of the site is not open to the public. The only part of

Fort George to survive the attacks was the stone **powder magazine,** today the oldest building in the town. Eight of the original wooden buildings have been reconstructed and are open to visitors. They include a **barracks, officers' quarters, guardhouse, kitchens,** and **blockhouses.** Furnished in authentic period decor, they present a vivid picture of the contrasting living conditions of the different military ranks.

**Playing the role of British infantry, War of 1812 reenactors at Fort George fire in line, the best formation for musket volleys.**

The officers' quarters were significantly more comfortable than the barracks housing the ordinary soldiers and the few women and children who lived in the fort. Protecting the inner buildings are **six earthen** and **wooden bastions,** connected by a **wooden palisade.** A dry ditch borders the palisade.

A highlight of the fort is the **stone tunnel** linking the original stone **powder magazine** to the **octagonal blockhouse,** near the south palisade. Built in a natural ravine a safe distance from other buildings, the powder magazine has buttressed bomb- and fireproof walls. Stairs inside the blockhouse lead up to the **loopholes,** which provide a soldier's-eye-view of the surrounding landscape and fort buildings.

**Brock's Bastion** in the northwest corner of the site was the original burial place of Maj. Gen. Sir Isaac Brock, the senior commander of British forces in Upper Canada, and his aide-de-camp, John Macdonell, who died during the Battle of Queenston Heights in October 1812 (see p. 43). Their remains were later moved back to Queenston Heights. A stone memorial and plaque mark Brock's first resting place at Fort George.

(see p. 43)

## Nearby & Noteworthy

✳ **BUTLER'S BARRACKS** After the War of 1812, the British built Butler's Barracks to replace Fort George, on a site west of the old fort. Four of the buildings are 19th-century structures, housing the Lincoln and Welland Regimental Museum. The British Indian Department was also here; a plaque marks the Indian Council House where important meetings were held between the British and their Native Nations allies during the War of 1812. *Queen's Parade, Niagara-on-the-Lake, ON, www.parkscanada.gc.ca*

✳ **NAVY HALL** An important supply facility for all the British forts in the Niagara region, and also used as a dining hall for the officers of Fort George, this collection of buildings was destroyed by U.S. forces during the War of 1812. The British rebuilt it after the war. Although the hall itself is not open to the public, the grounds are worth visiting for their views of Fort Niagara. *305 Ricardo Street, Niagara-on-the-Lake, ON, www.parkscanada.gc.ca*

Costumed staff and volunteers bring the fort's history alive and describe the day-to-day existence of the soldiers stationed here 200 years ago. Cannon are mounted on the bastions, some trained on Fort Niagara.

The fort frequently holds historical reenactments, special events, and themed tours, as well as learning experiences when children get to wear their own redcoat. The interactive **War of 1812 exhibit** explores the conflict from American, Canadian, and Haudenosaunee perspectives, while the **sound and light show** "Flames of War" dramatizes the 1813 battle at Fort George.

The ghost tour is especially popular on summer evenings, when black-caped guides take visitors through the dimly lit fort and relate tales of supernatural sightings.

During the day, musket and artillery displays entertain visitors. Fife and drum corps provide the sounds of 1812, while the officers' kitchen prepares baked goods according to 19th-century recipes. ∎

**51 Queen's Parade, Niagara-on-the-Lake, ON • 905-468-6614 • www.parkscanada.gc.ca • $ • Closed Nov. to April, except weekends in April and Nov.**

# »QUEENSTON HEIGHTS NATIONAL HISTORIC SITE

**High above the Niagara River, opposite Lewiston, New York, Queenston Heights was the setting for the first major battle on Canadian soil. The Battle of Queenston Heights, in October, 1812, ended in a British victory and the capture of nearly a thousand U.S. troops, but Maj. Gen. Sir Isaac Brock, the commander of British forces in Upper Canada died in the battle, along with his second in command.**

In the autumn of 1813, as American Maj. Gen. Stephen Van Rensselaer gathered thousands of militia and regulars in Lewiston on the New York side of the Niagara River, the British braced themselves for an attack somewhere on the Niagara frontier. Before dawn on October 13, Lt. Col. Solomon Van Rensselaer, cousin of Stephen Van Rensselaer, led a flotilla of boats carrying hundreds of U.S. soldiers across the Niagara River to Queenston. As the Americans began to disembark, the British bombarded them with musket and cannon fire. Those still in boats also came under fire and some were swept downriver by the current. The Americans returned fire, pushing the British back from Queenston landing. However, the heavy firing injured Van Rensselaer soon after his arrival on shore.

Planning to outflank the British, U.S. Capt. John Wool led a group of men up a fishermen's pathway behind the battery guarding the portage route from Queenston to Fort Chippawa. From the protection of the woods at the top of the path, Wool's army fired on the small British defense at

the cannon. The Americans gained control of the Heights and drove the British back. Brock, who had raced to the Heights from Fort George, retreated with his men and considered his position. He decided on a swift counterattack, but as he began his ascent of the Heights, he was fatally

**Reenactors stand in front of Brock Monument, commemorating the British general killed at Queenston Heights.**

wounded by an infantryman firing a musket. John Macdonell, Brock's aide-de-camp, followed with a second charge but he, too, was mortally wounded.

Confident that the Americans could keep control of the Heights with more support, Stephen Van Rensselaer sent orders for the remaining men to cross the river and climb to the Heights. But the largely untrained militiamen were not obliged to fight on foreign soil and refused to join the battle.

Back on the Heights, the Americans, now under the command of Lt. Col. Winfield Scott, were attacked by British reinforcements. A force of 100 Grand River warriors led by Mohawk captains John Norton and John Brant began the assault and destabilized the Americans. They were backed by militia from York and Lincoln counties, including 40 men of the Colored Corps, an African-American militia unit. Arriving on the scene from Fort George, British Maj. Gen. Roger Hale Sheaffe led an additional group of militia and soldiers up to the Heights and ordered a charge on the Americans. Trapped between the cliffs and the British, the Americans surrendered. The British took 958 prisoners, including Scott.

**The battlefield today** The site of the battle is beautifully landscaped, with gardens,

This engraving based on a sketch by James Dennis (1796–1855) shows American troops crossing the Niagara River by boat to attack the British base at Queenston Heights.

wooded areas, pavilions, and markers for significant sites. The park follows the line of the Niagara escarpment and offers fine views of Lake Ontario and the river.

A self-guided walking tour of the battleground begins at **Brock's Monument,** where Brock and John Macdonell are buried. The tour highlights five decisive points in the battle, each marked by a bronze plaque describing what took place there. A plaque marks the fatal wounding of Macdonell, while a cairn at the foot of the hill marks the spot where Brock was killed. There are plans

to build a memorial to the Native allies who fought in the war.

The site has a number of other 1812 plaques and memorials. On the edge of the park is a large **stone dedicated to Laura Secord,** an inhabitant of Queenston who is popularly credited with warning British forces of a possible U.S. attack at DeCew House (see p. 49) in June 1813. The stone has an oval plaque with a relief portrait of the heroine. The low wall behind the monument provides sweeping views over the river.

**Fort Drummond** Not far from Brock's monument are the ruins of Fort Drummond, a small, square fortification built in 1814 to protect the portage road from Chippawa to Queenston. Also near Brock's monument is a **plaque commemorating the Colored Corps.** Commanded by a white British leader, many of them had traveled north from the United States. ■

**14184 Niagara Pkwy., Queenston, ON • 905-468-4257 • www.parkscanda.gov.ca • Brock's Monument closed Labor Day to April**

### Nearby & Noteworthy

✳ **LAURA SECORD HOMESTEAD** The meticulously restored home of the Canadian heroine offers a glimpse of ordinary life in 1812. Costumed interpreters provide information. *29 Queenston St., Queenston, ON, www.niagaraparks.com*

## » BATTLE OF STONEY CREEK NATIONAL HISTORIC SITE

Modern-day Hamilton, Ontario, surrounds a well-preserved area commemorating the Battle of Stoney Creek, fought on June 6, 1813. Beginning with a surprise British attack on the U.S. encampment, the battle turned into a significant British victory that paved the way for the successful defense of Upper Canada. Covering 32 acres (13 ha), the parkland includes some of the original battle sites, Battlefield House, where American officers were billeted, and the Battlefield Monument. There is also a cemetery with memorials to some of the people who played key roles in the battle. In June each year, Stoney Creek is the setting for one of the largest War of 1812 reenactments in North America.

After the capture of Fort George (see p. 40) at the end of May 1813, the British retreated west to Burlington Heights, now in the modern city of Hamilton. They established a new base, with senior officers occupying a brick cottage while soldiers and some families made do with sheds, barns, and tents. It was here that beleaguered British soldiers from Fort George and Fort Erie awaited the advancement of the American troops.

Around 3,400 U.S. soldiers advanced on Burlington Heights. On June 5, 1813, under the orders of American Gen. Henry Dearborn, Brig. Gen. John Chandler and Brig. Gen. William Winder set out separately with their troops, meeting at

Forty Mile (present day Grimsby, Ontario) and continuing to Stoney Creek, where they set up camp for the night. Here, the two commanding officers based their headquarters in the home of the widow Mary Jones Gage.

There are varying accounts of how British Brig. Gen. John Vincent learned of the American position at Stoney Creek. A popular tale, discredited by most local historians, is that a local teenager called Billy Green infiltrated the U.S. camp using the password—"Wil-Hen-Har." Other accounts credit British scouts or Lt. Col. John Harvey, Vincent's second-in-command, with obtaining the crucial intelligence. However the news reached the British, they took advantage of the darkness to attack. John Harvey, aided by a small corps of Native allies led by Mohawk war captain John Norton, approached the U.S. camp in the early hours of June 6.

The stealthy advance surprised the American sentries, who quickly fell to bayonet attacks as the British moved toward the camp. But the U.S. soldiers in the camp heard the sound of musket fire and hurriedly organized themselves against the attack. As chaos ensued, many troops fell on both sides, scattering the battlefield with wounded and dying men.

The dark night made it difficult to distinguish one side from the other. The British seized the American artillery at Smith's Knoll and took both General Winder and Chandler prisoner. This left the

**The annual commemoration of the Battle of Stoney Creek takes place on the first weekend in June and includes artillery demonstrations, fireworks, and a reenactment of the battle.**

U.S. forces under Col. James Burn, who led their retreat, first to Forty Mile, where they were shelled by British naval forces on Lake Ontario and attacked on land by Native warriors and Canadian militia, and finally to Fort George (see pp. 40–42).

## Battlefield House Museum and Park

Visitors to this well-preserved historic site can tour the grounds, explore Battlefield House, and take in the view from the observation deck of the monument overlooking the park. **Battlefield House** was the home of Mary Jones Gage, where the U.S. officers were billeted. A Georgian colonial structure with a wide front veranda, it has 19th-century furniture and decor in each of the main rooms and an original stencil in the front entrance hall. Upstairs, in a 1926 addition, is a military exhibit, with memorabilia and information on the Battle of Stoney Creek. Another restored home in Battlefield Park, **Grandview,** was moved to the park from Stoney Creek in 1999. It houses a gift shop.

Soldiers from both sides of the Battle of Stoney Creek are commemorated by a cairn in Smith's Knoll.

*Nearby & Noteworthy*

✳ **STONEY CREEK CEMETERY** To the east of Battlefield Park, across Centennial Parkway South, this cemetery contains a monument to three key figures in the Battle of Stoney Creek: Billy Green, who purportedly informed the British that the Americans were about to attack; his brother-in-law, Isaac Corman, from whom Billy reputedly learned the password to the U.S. camp; and Colonel John Harvey. *2860 King St., Hamilton, ON*

On the ridge above the house is the **Battlefield Monument,** built in Tudor Gothic Revival style in 1913. Steps from the house lead up to the 100-foot-tall (30 m) structure—its height a reference to the century of peace between Canada and the United States at the time it was built. The monument features dedications and a plaque detailing the events of June 6, 1813. The view from the observation deck extends beyond the park to Stoney Creek and the expanse of Lake Ontario.

**Smith's Knoll** Just north of Battlefield Park, on the other side of King Street West, is Smith's Knoll. In 1813, the Americans set up their guns here. In the late 19th century, the farmer's son, Allen Smith, unearthed human remains, bits of cloth, and buttons bearing British and American insignia. These are buried in the **Soldiers' Plot,** consecrated in 1908. It is marked by a **fieldstone cairn,** dedicated in 1910, commemorating those who fell in the battle. ∎

Battlefield House Museum and Park, 77 King St. W, Stoney Creek, ON
• 905-662-8458
• www.battle fieldhouse.ca
• $ • Closed Mon.

## >> BATTLE OF BEAVER DAMS NATIONAL HISTORIC SITE

After their defeat at the Battle of Stoney Creek on June 6, 1813, the Americans retreated to Fort George where they made plans for another attack. Meanwhile, British troops had regrouped at three posts in the Niagara peninsula, including one called DeCew House in the town of Thorold. The former home of a loyalist captured in Philadelphia, DeCew House was under the command of Lt. James FitzGibbon and used as a supply depot as well as an army base. On June 23, 1813, the American Lt. Col. Charles Boerstler set out from Fort George to Queenston, leading an army of several hundred troops. The Americans arrived near the site that evening and planned their surprise attack for the following morning.

Meanwhile, FitzGibbon received visitors to DeCew House. On June 22, Laura Secord from Queenston, escorted by two Grand River warriors, brought news of U.S. maneuvers. Other local inhabitants, British army scouts and French Canadian officer Dominique Ducharme, leading a party of Native allies, also brought word back to FitzGibbon of American advances.

On the morning of June 24, Native Nations scouts and militia cavalry reported that the Americans were moving from Queenston to St. David's and then toward DeCew House in Thorold. From the woods outside Thorold, more than 400 Mohawk and Caughnawaga warriors fired at Boerstler's American forces as they tried to advance. The U.S. troops, unprepared for the onslaught, were defeated within a few hours and began to withdraw. FitzGibbon and his small group arrived before the retreat got fully under way and convinced

### Quick History

Born in 1775 in Massachusetts, Laura Secord (born Ingersoll) immigrated to Upper Canada with her family in 1795. Two years later she married James Secord, a Loyalist (an American who sought to remain loyal to the British crown after the Revolutionary War). Her first act in the War of 1812 was to rescue her wounded husband from the battlefield at Queenston Heights. In June 1813, U.S. troops occupied Queenston and Laura learned of American plans to scout out the British position at DeCew House. She traveled a perilous 20 miles (32 km) on foot to warn Lt. James FitzGibbon.

Boerstler that he was outnumbered and could only be made safe from the wrath of the warriors if he surrendered.

The Battle of Beaver Dams took place around the intersection of Old Thorold and Davis Roads, but the landscape has changed dramatically since that time. Both the Welland Canal and the Thorold Tunnel cut through the battleground, leaving little of the original site. For this reason, the large stone cairn that once marked the site of the battle now sits in the **Battle of Beaverdams Park** in Thorold. A bronze plaque recounts the events of June 24, 1813.

The other memorial in the park marks the gravesite of 16 American soldiers originally interred at the battle site. Although a fire destroyed **DeCew House** in 1950, some lower walls and fireplaces remain and a plaque outlines its history.

**Davis Rd., Thorold, ON • www.historic places.ca**

# »Old Fort Niagara State Historic Site

Fort Niagara was a base for U.S. campaigns in the Niagara region. Occupying a bluff at the mouth of the Niagara River, overlooking Lake Ontario, the fort had considerable strategic value for forces wishing to control the portage corridor between Lake Ontario and Lake Erie. On the opposite bank of the river, facing the American fort, stood Fort George, captured by U.S. forces in May 1813 (see pp. 40–42). In December, British forces, under the newly appointed commander in Upper Canada, Lt. Gen. Gordon Drummond, set about retaking Fort George and then destroying Fort Niagara.

By December 1813, just over 100 U.S. troops remained at Fort George. Learning that the British intended to retake the fort, the American commander, Brig. Gen. George McClure, ordered a retreat to Fort Niagara on the opposite side of river, after burning the fort and the Town of Niagara.

Once again in control of Fort George, the British gathered troops for their assault on Fort Niagara. Late on the night of December 18, Col. John Murray led more than 550 men across the river in two stages. Poor outer defenses, which had not been repaired since the earlier battles, made it relatively easy for the first wave of British troops to gain entry to the fort.

While some Americans sought refuge in the south redoubt and barracks, from where they could fire on the British invaders, they were eventually forced to surrender. The British bayoneted any who resisted capture of the redoubt, and on December 19 the fort was captured. The Americans suffered many casualties during the battle, including hundreds who were taken prisoner.

When British Lt. Gen. Gordon Drummond arrived in person to take control of Fort Niagara, he ordered raids on American villages and towns, including Lewiston and Buffalo, in retribution for the burning of the Town of Niagara (see p. 40), ordered by General McClure. As a consequence, the village of the Tuscarora Nation above Lewiston was also burned.

**The fort today** The restoration of Fort Niagara took place in the late 1920s and early 1930s. Most of the work aimed to bring the fort back to its 18th-century appearance, though 19th-century additions, such as the river defenses, were retained. In Old Fort Niagara the "House of Peace," built

## Don't Miss

✳ **U.S. Garrison Flag** One of Fort Niagara's most treasured artifacts is the U.S. garrison flag captured during the British attack on the fort in 1813. General Drummond took the prized flag back to his ancestral home in Scotland, where it remained until 1994.

by the French in 1727, and now known as the **French Castle,** is one of the oldest buildings in the Great Lakes. Used as a trading house, where Haudenosaunee bartered furs for manufactured goods, it had storerooms, quarters, and a chapel, but its added defensive role is evident in its distinctive machicolated dormers, which provided outlook points and space to fire at invading enemies. When the British captured the fort in 1759, during the French and Indian War, they added a stockade, two stone redoubts, and a new bakehouse and storehouse.

A tour of the French Castle includes the **soldiers' barracks, chapel, officers'**

**quarters,** and **trading room**, all furnished in the style of the period. Six other buildings on the site include the **powder magazine,** built in 1757, and the two **redoubts** built in 1770 and 1771. The **river defenses,** built in 1839, overlook the river and Fort George in Ontario. Living history exhibits and events re-create the War of 1812 and the history of the Tuscarora people.

In addition, Old Fort Niagara holds a large collection of **military artifacts** dating from the 17th century to the 1960s, when the fort ceased to have a military function. It includes artillery and weapons, military uniforms, books, and photographs. ■

**4 Scott Ave., Youngstown, NY • 761-745-7611 • www.nysparks.com • $**

**The French Castle, the oldest part of the Fort Niagara complex, dating from 1726**

## » Battle of Chippawa National Historic Site

Following the American capture of Fort Erie (see p. 54), U.S. troops continued to advance into the Niagara peninsula. On July 4, 1814, American Brig. Gen. Winfield Scott led an army of 1,300 soldiers to Street's Creek (now Usshers Creek, Niagara Falls, Ontario). Scott's superior, Gen. Jacob Brown, arrived that night with another 2,000 troops. Meanwhile, British forces under Maj. Gen. Phineas Riall moved south from Fort George, first to Fort Chippawa and then to Street's Creek. Riall did not realize that Fort Erie had fallen so quickly and believed that U.S. troops continued to lay siege to the fort. Underestimating the size of the U.S. forces, he planned to block their advance at Chippawa.

The battle began in the early morning of July 5 with skirmishing between British militia and their Native Nations allies in the forest next to Samuel Street's farm. Riall ordered successive attacks on the American line, but with 1,000 more men, the U.S. line outflanked the British. Surprised by the skillful maneuvers—the British had thought the U.S. soldiers in gray coats were untrained militia—and suffering heavy casualties, Riall ordered a retreat, signaling a U.S. victory.

Today, **Chippawa Battlefield Park** preserves the battle site on 300 acres (121 ha) of open field and wooded areas.

### Quick History

Around 500 Native warriors from the Buffalo Creek reservation near Buffalo, New York, aided the American assault at Chippawa. They had a bloody fight defeating John Norton and his Grand River warriors, and as a consequence most of the Haudenosaunee decided on a mutual withdrawal from the war.

A **memorial** to the battle, erected in 2001, is built with limestone from Old Fort Niagara. Markers detail the site of the first strike on July 5, the U.S. advancement, the battle on the plain, the final stages, and the aftermath.

**9233 Niagara Parkway, Niagara Falls, ON • www.niagaraparks.com**

## » Lundy's Lane National Historic Site

Not long after the Battle of Chippawa, the Americans and British met again, this time just north on Lundy's Lane, a country road within earshot of the roar of Niagara Falls. General Brown had pursued the British on their retreat to Fort George, planning to lay siege to the fort with the help of naval forces. However, when Commodore Isaac Chauncey's Lake Ontario squadron failed to arrive, Brown and his troops retired to Street's Creek on the other side of the Chippawa River. The British followed, and took up a position on high ground at Lundy's Lane.

Meanwhile, Brown had been planning to march up Lundy's Lane and attack the British at Burlington Heights in order to isolate the British garrison of Niagara. To do this, he needed to dislodge the British forces from Lundy's Lane. He ordered Brig. Gen. Winfield Scott to bring more men.

Scott and his soldiers marched along the Portage Road and arrived near Lundy's Lane in the early evening. Spying

**Lt. Gen. Gordon Drummond led several counterattacks at Lundy's Lane, but did not secure a decisive British victory.**

the British on the ridge, the Americans attacked with force, sparking an equally ferocious British retaliation. As the battle raged, the Americans captured injured Riall. Drummond and Brown arrived with reinforcements for both sides, but darkness fell and it became difficult to see. During the chaos, the Americans captured the British guns, forcing the British to retreat to the other side of the hill. Drummond attempted to recapture the guns, but failed.

Brown and Scott, both seriously injured and their troops exhausted, called for a withdrawal to Fort Chippawa. They retreated farther, to Fort Erie, followed a month later by Drummond. The battle ended with heavy casualties on both sides and no clear victor.

Lundy's Lane is now a busy street in Niagara Falls and private property covers much of the battlefield. However, visitors can tour **Drummond Hill Cemetery,** the focal point of the battle, and pick up a pamphlet outlining a walking tour of the site. Within the cemetery, a **stone cairn**

indicates the battleground, a monument marks the **grave of 22 British soldiers** killed, and a **commemorative wall** depicts scenes of the battle. The grave of Laura Secord, who may have warned British forces of a possible attack at DeCew House (see box, p. 49) is in the cemetery.

**Niagara Falls History Museum,** on Ferry Street, displays uniforms, weaponry, and documents from the war and runs events ranging from Regency-style English country dancing to nighttime walks of the cemetery led by a costumed guide.

6110 Lundy's Ln., Niagara Falls, ON
• www.historicplaces.ca; Niagara Falls History Museum, 5810 Ferry St., Niagara Falls, ON
• www.niagarafallshistorymuseum.ca • $
• Closed Mon.

---

### *Don't Miss*

✳ **BATTLE GROUND HOTEL MUSEUM** Opposite Drummond Hill Cemetery in Lundy's Lane is the former Fralick Tavern, a popular place to stay in the mid-19th century, when tourism to the Niagara Falls and the battlefields of 1812 began to take off. Now a museum, the tavern has been restored. Its collection includes many artifacts from the War of 1812. *5161 Lundy's Ln., Niagara Falls, ON, www.niagarafallshistorymuseum.ca*

## » *Fort Erie National Historic Site*

**The British built Fort Erie, in Upper Canada, to guard the entrance to the Niagara River from Lake Erie. The violent winter storms took their toll on two earlier forts situated on the edge of the river, so in the early 1800s the British constructed a new fort of local flint on higher ground. Although incomplete during the War of 1812, the fort was fiercely contested by the Americans and the British and was the scene of one of the bloodiest campaigns in the war.**

On May 27, 1813, after the American capture of Fort George, the British abandoned the unfinished Fort Erie, at the eastern end of Lake Erie, the far end of their defensive line, allowing U.S. troops to occupy it. But the Americans soon deserted the site, and returned to Fort George to reinforce their numbers there. Reoccupying Fort Erie in December 1813, the British set about strengthening the site, but continued to maintain only a small garrison here.

On July 3, 1814, the Americans returned to attack Fort Erie with more than 4,000 troops, forcing a quick surrender and taking almost 200 British prisoners. American Brig. Gen. Edmund Gaines and his troops improved the fort's defenses, extending the earthen walls and erecting a gun battery and palisade. Just over a month later, the British returned under Lt. Gen. Gordon Drummond and laid siege to the fort.

The first assault did not force an American surrender. Determined to follow through, Drummond decided to attack the fort in three waves and from three different directions, beginning in the early hours of August 15, 1814.

The Americans met the first attack with fierce retaliation and the second one with even more firepower. The number of British deaths mounted, as did the number of men wounded. Drummond's third column stormed the northeast bastion, and

Aerial view of Fort Erie, showing its star-shaped earthworks and lakeside position, with the visitor's center to the fore

captured a cannon that they then turned on the *redan* (projecting fortification in the surrounding wall).

In the exchange of fire, a powder magazine under the bastion ignited and exploded, destroying part of the barracks and killing or wounding hundreds of British troops simultaneously. In spite of the magnitude of the loss, Drummond persisted with the siege, though with smaller and less effective attacks.

Finally, on September 17, the Americans set out on an offensive campaign to capture the British batteries and succeeded in destroying two of them. Further fighting ensued during the sortie. Drummond lifted the siege on September 21, gathered his remaining men, and withdrew to Fort Chippawa. The siege had claimed more than 3,000 men, either wounded or killed,

more than any other campaign fought on Canadian soil. The Americans remained at Fort Erie until early November, when they retreated to Buffalo, destroying the fort before they left. Since most of the fort was in ruins, the British maintained only a sporadic presence there until 1823.

**Visiting the fort** Reconstruction of the fort began in 1937, and Old Fort Erie, restored to its 1814 appearance, opened to the public in 1939. During the reconstruction period, workers discovered a mass grave containing the remains of 150 British soldiers and three Americans who died during the siege of 1814. The monument to the siege marks the grave site and a **plaque** commemorates the fallen soldiers.

A closer look at the fort's 3-feet-thick (1 m) **curtain wall** reveals some original flintstone (darker) near the bottom. Step inside the gate to journey back to the 19th century. Costumed guides provide entertainment, such as **musket demonstrations,** and information on the fort's history. The **barracks, three powder magazines, officers' quarters,** and **kitchen,** all furnished in the style of early 19th-century military interiors, can be visited. A small number of women would have lived at the fort, to cook and launder for the troops.

The fort's **visitor center** features a movie theater, exhibits on American and British experiences of the battle, and cannonballs, muskets, and surgical instruments. A reenactment of the Siege of Fort Erie takes place on the second weekend in August. ■

**350 Lakeshore Rd., Fort Erie, ON • 905-871-0540 • www.niagaraparks.com • $ • Closed Nov. to April**

## » Fort Mississauga National Historic Site

By December 1813, the British had reclaimed Fort George and seized Fort Niagara across the river, but the war was far from over and the Niagara region of Upper Canada needed further defenses. Mississauga Point, named for the Native Nation that controlled Niagara in the 1770s, was considered the ideal position for a new fortification. It was just north of Fort George, at the mouth of the Niagara River. Work on the new fort began in spring 1814.

To make way for the new fortification, the 1804 Mississauga Point Lighthouse, the first lighthouse on the Great Lakes, was demolished. Fort Mississauga incorporates stones from the lighthouse as well as materials from the ruins of the Town of Niagara (Niagara-on-the-Lake). The square tower has thick, strong walls to protect the garrison from cannon fire, a single entryway, and several loopholes. The two brick-lined powder magazines were built into the earthworks to prevent their destruction from possible howitzer or mortar fire.

As the war-ravaged Fort George became more dilapidated, the British repositioned their garrison at Fort Mississauga. However, peace was declared in 1815 and the fort never faced attack, although its guns were fired in July 1814 when Brown's army advanced to Niagara to lay siege on the town. Although the British repaired and garrisoned the fort again after the Rebellion of 1837 and during the Fenian Raids in 1866, by the late 1860s the military had abandoned it. The Canadian Army used the grounds for training during the two World Wars.

Fort Mississauga is the only remaining example in Canada of a square tower with a star-shaped earthwork. Though there is no public access inside the tower, visitors can explore the grounds, including one of the **tunnels through the earthworks,** which leads to a view of Lake Ontario. Plaques detail the history of the fort. Visitors are required to follow a marked path that begins at the corner of Front and Simcoe Streets.

**223 Queen St., Niagara-on-the-Lake, ON • www.parkscanada.gc.ca**

**Watercolor of Fort Mississauga in 1840, showing the original tower and barracks. Fort Niagara is shown in the distance.**

## » OTHER SITES & PLAQUES

### ✤ BATTLE OF COOKS MILLS

A stone cairn and plaque mark the site of a skirmish that took place on October 19, 1814. Britain and the U.S. claimed victory. **Lyons Creek Rd., Welland, ON • www .historicplaces.ca**

### ✤ BATTLE OF FRENCHMAN'S CREEK NATIONAL HISTORIC SITE

A stone monument marks the site of a skirmish between U.S. and British troops on November 28, 1812. Landing under cover of darkness, the Americans planned to burn the bridge at Frenchman's Creek, in order to prevent the British from accessing Fort Erie. They succeeded in seizing the battery, but British reinforcements forced them to withdraw. **Niagara Pkwy., Fort Erie, ON • www.historicplaces.ca**

### ✤ BURLINGTON HEIGHTS

Following the attack on Fort George, the British retreated to Burlington Heights. Brig. Gen. John Vincent built a fortification here and gathered his troops for the Battle of Stoney Creek. In addition to a stone monument, a plaque in Hamilton Cemetery lies on some surviving earthworks. **Dundurn Park, York Blvd., Hamilton, ON • www.historicplaces.ca**

### ✤ BUTLER'S FARM

On July 8, 1813, the British set out to recover medical supplies buried at Two Mile Creek, near Fort George. When U.S. troops arrived, a battle ensued. Later in the day, Native Nations warriors hiding in the woods ambushed U.S. reinforcements, killing 22 American soldiers. **Butler's Burying Ground, Butler St., Niagara-on-the-Lake, ON • www.parkscanada.gc.ca**

### ✤ ENGAGEMENT AT THE FORTY

A stone monument and the Grimsby Bicentennial Peace Garden mark the site of a skirmish at Forty Mile Creek when U.S. forces were driven back to Fort George by the British Lake Ontario flotilla, Canadian Militia, and Haudenosaunee allies. **Elizabeth St., Grimsby, ON**

### ✤ FORT CHIPPAWA

A plaque near the entrance to King's Bridge Park in Niagara Falls marks the site of Fort Chippawa (also known as Fort Welland). The fort comprised a simple log blockhouse surrounded by a stockade. **7870 Niagara Pkwy., Niagara Falls, ON • www.ontarioplaques.com**

### ★ FORT SCHLOSSER

All that remains of Fort Schlosser, near the Niagara Falls, is its stone chimney, now in the grounds of the Carborundum Company (it can be seen from the Robert Moses State Parkway). The fort was built by the British but occupied by the U.S. during the War of 1812. The British captured the fort in 1813. **23 Acheson Dr., Niagara Falls, NY**

### ✤ NIAGARA-ON-THE-LAKE HISTORIC DISTRICT

Following the burning of Newark, now Niagara-on-the-Lake, the British rebuilt the town. Its restored and preserved buildings include the old apothecary and the court house. **Queen St., Niagara-on-the-Lake, ON • www .historicplaces.ca**

### ✤ VROOMAN'S BATTERY NATIONAL HISTORIC SITE

This was the site of a 24-pounder gun battery used by the British during the Battle of Queenston Heights. **Queenston, ON • www.historicplaces.ca**

Area
Enlarged

*Present-day Map*

**3**

C A N A D A

ONTARIO

Pembroke •

*Ottawa*

⊛ Ottawa

Prescott ◻

Ogdensburg
Battlefield

*Lake
Simcoe*

Barrie •

Kingston
Fortifications
NHS

The Escape of
H.M.S. *Royal George*

*St. Lawrence*

Brown
Mansion

• Watertown

Sackets Harbor
Battlefield State
Historic Site;
Sackets Harbor
Military Cemetery

Toronto •
Fort York NHS ◼

*L a k e   O n t a r i o*

Fort Ontario
State Historic Site

• Hamilton

Niagara Falls •

Rochester •

Syracuse •

• Buffalo

*Lake  Erie*

NEW YORK

Ithaca •

*Chautauqua
Lake*

U N I T E D    S T A T E S

• Jamestown

◼ National Historic Site (NHS)
◻ Other
• Present-day major city

0                    40 mi

0        40 km

*Present-day Map*

PENNSYLVANIA

# LAKE ONTARIO

The battle for supremacy over the Great Lakes drove the Americans and the British to build ships at a frantic pace. Both nations established their primary naval industries on the shores of Lake Ontario, the closest lake to the Atlantic. At the start of the war, the British Provincial Marine flotilla consisted of two brigs and five schooners. By contrast, the Americans had one 16-gun brig, U.S.S. *Oneida*, but they also purchased and armed merchant vessels. U.S. Commodore Isaac Chauncey expanded the yard at Sackets Harbor, New York, with the aim of enlarging America's freshwater fleet. In November 1812, the U.S. Navy launched the first American warship, U.S.S. *Madison*, of the Lake Ontario Squadron. The following March, Royal Navy Capt. James Lucas Yeo became commander of British naval forces on the lakes, and he, too, supervised the building of bigger warships. Nonetheless, a full-scale decisive naval battle never materialized on Lake Ontario.

**3**

Uniform of a British militia officer serving in the War of 1812

## » FORT YORK NATIONAL HISTORIC SITE

The Lieutenant Governor of Upper Canada, John Graves Simcoe, established York and its defenses in 1793 on the northwest shore of Lake Ontario. In 1796, York, now Toronto, became the provincial capital of Upper Canada. Simcoe commissioned blockhouses, barracks, and gun batteries, but he did not fortify the site further in favor of reinforcing Kingston, the eastern entrance to the Great Lakes. In 1800, the British added Government House to Fort York, and in 1811, as war with the United States became increasingly likely, they strengthened the fort with a circular battery and wall. Even so, the fort and its small garrison were ill-prepared for the intensity and volume of the U.S. attack that was to come in 1813.

Aware of the strong defenses at Kingston and Burlington Heights, the Americans decided to target the poorly defended Fort York on their first combined army and naval strike. On April 27, 1813, Commodore Isaac Chauncey's fleet delivered 1,700 troops from the American base in Sackets Harbor, New York. Brig. Gen. Zebulon Pike, a renowned American explorer and soldier, led the troops on land.

Unsure where the Americans would disembark, the British Maj. Gen. Roger Hale Sheaffe divided his small force of regulars, militia, and Native warriors into smaller units, sending just a few hundred men to guard the area west of the fort. In fact, the Americans landed west, at present-day Sunnyside Beach. A force mainly consisting of Anishinaabeg warriors confronted the American troops, but heavy gunfire from the U.S. schooners covered the American riflemen as they advanced.

Unable to withstand the onslaught, the defenders retreated into the woods and

A watercolor of Fort York before its destruction in 1813. The British rebuilt the fort later in the year on the opposite side of Garrison Creek.

toward the western battery of Fort York. As the British rallied around the battery, its traveling magazine blew up, killing about 20 men and forcing a further retreat into the fort. The U.S. forces continued their assault on land and from the water.

General Sheaffe soon realized the Americans were taking control of the battle and that his small garrison could not withstand the attack. He decided to thwart them by setting alight the unfinished frigate, H.M.S. *Sir Isaac Brock*, naval storehouses, and the fort's main powder magazine, containing 200 barrels of gunpowder and other munitions. The explosion killed or wounded more than 200 men. A large boulder from

*Don't Miss*

✷ **THE OFFICERS' BRICK BARRACKS**
The cellar of this building in Fort York contains the original 1815 kitchen. The oldest kitchen in Toronto, it includes the original drainage system, storage for wine, and two fireproof money vaults installed in 1838, during the Upper Canada Rebellion.

the blast crushed many of them, including the U.S.'s General Pike and a British sergeant. Both men died of their injuries. Meanwhile, Sheaffe retreated to Kingston, leaving the local militia to surrender to Maj. Gen. Henry Dearborn.

For the next six days, the Americans occupied York, and soldiers looted and set fire to public buildings, including the provincial parliament, Government House, and library. The U.S. forces captured supplies and artillery in a second raid on York on July 31.

Later that year, the British rebuilt Fort York, adding fortifications, blockhouses, and new barracks. They stayed there for

the rest of the war. British and Canadian troops occupied the fort on and off until 1932, after which the City of Toronto restored the fort and opened it to the public in 1934.

**Fort York today** The fort occupies more than 43 acres (17 ha) of preserved green space, surrounded by Toronto's towering buildings and a crisscross of inner city transportation routes. Originally the fort was on the shores of Lake Ontario, but land reclamation over the centuries means that it now sits several hundred yards north of the shoreline.

South of the fort, near the shore, a plaque in **Coronation Park** marks the second landing of American troops in July 1813. Another plaque on **The Esplanade** indicates the site of the original parliament buildings that were burned down in the aftermath of the attack on Fort York.

The fort contains Canada's largest collection of original War of 1812 structures, and a visit to the fort offers an authentic experience of 19th-century fort life. The buildings date back to the British reconstruction between 1813 and 1815, though the earthworks at the west gate and the circular battery date from 1805. Among the restored places to tour are the **soldiers' barracks** and the more comfortable **officers' barracks,** both built of brick in 1815. The officers' barracks, designed for three senior officers, includes a bedroom, sitting room, kitchen, pantries,

## Quick History

**N**ative warriors lent their support and skills to the British forces defending York. Mississauga and Chippawa soldiers were among the first to fight the Americans as they disembarked at Sunnyside Beach. In all, some 8,000–10,000 Native warriors fought on either the British or U.S. side in the war.

wine cellar, and mess room, plus quarters for two servants, all furnished in the style of the period. Other areas of interest are a **stone magazine,** an 1813 **blockhouse** containing an artillery exhibit, and the **kitchen garden,** modeled on a Georgian garden with raised vegetable beds.

In summer, there are daily demonstrations by the **Fort York Guard** as well as regular special events. The Guards play drums, perform drills, and fire the cannon.

Archaeologists at Fort York have excavated a wealth of artifacts, many of which are on display. Changing exhibits feature original and reproduction military items such as uniforms, tools, musical instruments, and weapons. There is also a book of remembrance—*Finding the Fallen*—listing the names of American, British, and Native Nations soldiers who lost their lives at Fort York in 1813.

**Military cemetery** As part of a visit to Fort York, a side trip to **Victoria Memorial Square,** a few blocks northeast, is recommended. This is the site of Toronto's first **military cemetery.** The site is the resting place of hundreds of soldiers and civilians connected with the fort over the course of its long history. A memorial commemorates those who died during the War of 1812. ■

**250 Fort York Blvd., Toronto, ON • www.fort york.ca • 416-392-6907 • $**

## ›› KINGSTON FORTIFICATIONS

The French set up a military and trading post at Kingston in 1663, recognizing the site's strategic value at the eastern entrance to the Great Lakes from the St. Lawrence River. The British took over in the mid-18th century, and in the 1790s they built a dockyard and a blockhouse on Point Frederick.

The British inland naval service, the Provincial Marines, established their headquarters at Kingston and launched their flagship, H.M.S. *Royal George*, from here in 1809. In order to defend the town and the shipyard, they also erected batteries on both sides of Point Frederick, at Point Mississauga and Point Henry.

In November 1812, U.S. Commodore Isaac Chauncey set his sights on destroying the guns and naval stores at Kingston. Sailing on board the U.S.S. *Oneida*, he approached Kingston from the west, leading a fleet of seven ships. Catching sight of the *Royal George*, the American flotilla gave chase, coming under fire itself at Point Frederick. By the day's end, the Americans had captured a British schooner. The long gun had exploded on the U.S.S. *Pert*, but there were few casualties. The battle demonstrated the U.S. Navy's growing strength.

Following the attack, the British reinforced their defenses by adding another blockhouse at Point Frederick and building Fort Henry, but the Americans did not seriously threaten Kingston again.

Today, the **Royal Military College** dominates Point Frederick, surrounded by post-1812 buildings, including the **Stone Frigate,** built in 1820 for storage and training purposes. In 1817, Britain and the United States signed the Rush-Bagot Agreement. This treaty, named for Secretary of State, Richard Rush, and Sir Charles

**The Fort Henry Guard in the uniforms of British soldiers, 1867**

Bagot, the British minister in Washington, limited the building of warships on the Great Lakes and Lake Champlain. A plaque near the Stone Frigate honors the agreement.

The **martello towers** (see p. 93) date from 1846 and the **Fort Frederick tower** houses a museum. Across Navy Bay is **Fort Henry,** built by the British in 1836 to replace the 1812 fort. Inside, the **Fort Henry Guard** re-creates 19th-century military life. Near the fort's entrance is a **memorial** to the Provincial Marine and Royal Navy seamen who served in the War of 1812.

**Point Frederick and Point Henry, Kingston, ON**
• www.historicplaces.ca • Fort Henry • $

## ≫SACKETS HARBOR BATTLEFIELD STATE HISTORIC SITE

At the start of the war, the U.S. Navy boosted its small fleet by purchasing and arming merchant vessels, but it quickly became clear that it would require purpose-built warships. Sackets Harbor, a tiny village on the northeastern shore of Lake Ontario, with a deepwater harbor, became the U.S. Navy's headquarters on the Great Lakes, as well as the site of a major shipyard and Army defensive installations. The British viewed the town as a prime military target, but an initial attack in 1812 was repulsed by U.S.S. *Oneida*.

Almost a year after the first assault on Sackets Harbor, British commander-in-chief, Lt. Gen. Sir George Prévost, ordered a fresh attack. Reconnaissance revealed that the U.S. squadron had sailed, leaving the harbor only lightly defended. On May 27, 1813, the British seized their chance.

From Kingston, Commodore James Lucas Yeo led a fleet of two brigs and three sloops carrying 870 men and landed at Sackets Harbor. Their objective was to destroy the shipyard and any ships under construction. If successful, the British would seize control of Lake Ontario and gain an advantage over America's fledgling freshwater navy.

### Quick History

In May 1814, British forces tried to intercept a U.S. convoy taking supplies from Oswego to Sackets Harbor. However, the British were ambushed by a combined force of American troops and Oneida warriors at Big Sandy Creek, halfway between the two ports. The battle forced the British back but they continued to blockade Lake Ontario. To evade the blockade, U.S. volunteers made an arduous overland journey to deliver a ship's cable to Sackets Harbor. Today, three memorials in Sackets Harbor, Smithville (NY), and Ellisburg (NY) mark the "Trail of the Great Rope."

The British landed on Horse Island, just west of Sackets Harbor, on May 29. Warned of the impending onslaught, Brig. Gen. Jacob Brown of the New York militia had assembled a force of 1,400 regular soldiers, militia, and Native warriors from the Oneida Nation. They tried to fend off the British at the causeway but, intimidated by the ferocity of the British assault and cannon fire, many ran away.

The British met a small force of U.S. regulars outside the village. The fighting lasted more than two hours. Mistakenly believing the Americans had surrendered, U.S. acting Lt. John Drury set fire to some storehouses and the

1812 naval reenactors in Sackets Harbor. Protected by the narrow inlet of Black River Bay, the harbor was ideal for a naval base.

unfinished U.S.S. *General Pike*. At the same time, however, the British believed that U.S. reinforcements were coming. This, along with lack of wind, convinced General Prévost to order a British retreat.

After the battle, the Americans strengthened their defenses, but the British did not attempt another attack on Sackets Harbor. Shipbuilding remained a priority for the Americans in 1814, and the Navy launched U.S.S. *Superior*, a 66-gun frigate, on May 1 that year. After the war, the U.S. Navy retained control of the shipyard.

**Exploring Sackets Harbor** There are traces of two War of 1812 fortifications—**Fort Kentucky** and **Fort Pike**—as well as several plaques, markers, and other buildings to explore. The self-guided **battlefield trail** connects to a **War of 1812 trail** through the village. The home of Augustus Sacket, the town's founder, which was built in 1801, is now a **visitor center** (301 W. Main St.). The historic **Navy Yard** includes 19th-century buildings such as the Lieutenant's House and the Commandant's House, the latter restored to its 1860s appearance. In summer, living history demonstrations and costumed interpreters bring the site alive. ■

Battlefield Site, 504 W. Main St., Sackets Harbor, NY • www.nysparks.com/historic-sites • $ • Buildings closed early Sept. to late May

## » Ogdensburg Battlefield

The Upper St. Lawrence River was a crucial transportation route to Upper Canada, and Prescott, midway between Montreal and Kingston, was a vital British port, fortified from 1813 by Fort Wellington (see pp. 81–83). Directly opposite Prescott stood the American town of Ogdensburg. Its defenses included the ruinous Fort Presentation, built by the French in 1749, and an incomplete new fortification, Fort Oswegatchie. Keen to sever the British supply routes, the Americans obstructed the passage of bateaux and Durham boats on the St. Lawrence whenever possible.

In the early months of the war, the two sides exchanged fire across the river. In October 1812, the British attacked Ogdensburg, but U.S. troops forced them back. During the months that followed, U.S. forces under Capt. Benjamin Forsyth made several raids across the river, including one on Elizabethtown (now Brockville) in early February 1813.

Though unauthorized by his commander-in-chief, British Gen. Sir George Prévost, Lt. Col. George MacDonnell led a raid on Ogdensburg on February 22. Hundreds of British troops marched from Prescott across the frozen river and advanced on the town. Though hampered by heavy snow, they captured the redan battery on the waterfront on the northern side of Ogdensburg and continued into town while another flank marched, unsuccessfully, toward Fort Presentation. Forsyth attempted to defend his position but, realizing he was outnumbered, ordered a retreat to Sackets Harbor (see pp. 64–65). MacDonnell then commanded his men to burn the U.S. barracks and two schooners. The British left Ogdensburg loaded with supplies.

The Mohawk community of Akwesasne some 40 miles away was torn apart by the war. Straddling the St. Lawrence River near Cornwall, Ontario, their loyalties were divided, some aiding both sides.

A bridge now connects Ogdensburg and Prescott, making it easy to visit both sites in one day. Historic plaques commemorate Ogdensburg's **Battlefield,** now part of the downtown area. A self-guided walk begins at City Hall and links the historic sites. A brochure detailing the walk is available from the city's Chamber of Commerce. Other places to see are the monument and plaques at the site of **Fort Presentation, Lighthouse Point,** and the old **Custom House** at 127 North Water Street, where soldiers sought refuge during the battle. ■

**Ogdensburg Chamber of Commerce, 1 Bridge Plaza, Ogdensburg, NY • www.ogdensburg.org**

---

### Quick History

**D**uring the war the standard infantry musket for U.S. and British troops was a muzzle loading, flintlock single-shot firearm that could only be fired a few times a minute by the best trained soldiers and was inaccurate beyond 30 yards (27 m). The most effective way to fight with such weapons was to line your troops up in tight masses to fire volleys. Other infantrymen used the smoothbore or later the Brown Bess or the Indian Pattern musket introduced in 1814.

## »FORT ONTARIO STATE HISTORIC SITE

A crucial American military depot on Lake Ontario during the War of 1812, Fort Ontario supplied Sackets Harbor (see p. 64–65), the main American Army and Navy base and the center for U.S. shipbuilding on the lakes. However, the Americans failed to foresee Fort Ontario's strategic importance before the outbreak of war and did not reinforce the stronghold in time for a British attack on the U.S. supply chain in May 1814.

Four forts have occupied the banks of the Oswego River in Oswego, New York. The first, built by the British in 1755, was the Fort of the Six Nations. The French destroyed it the following year, building Fort Ontario in 1759. The British deserted the fort during the American Revolution, and U.S. troops destroyed it in 1778. But the British viewed Oswego's location overlooking Lake Ontario as a useful base in their continuing dispute with the United States. In 1782, they rebuilt the fort for a third time, but agreed to turn it over to the Americans in 1796 to comply with the conditions of Jay's Treaty, an agreement to

**The current fort dates from the 1840s, but parts of the earthworks were built in 1759.**

avert the resumption of hostilities between Britain and the U.S. The Americans allowed the fort to fall into disrepair.

**Strategic importance** With the outbreak of war in 1812, Fort Ontario became an important American storage depot for goods brought up by river from the Atlantic seaboard and the Hudson Valley. From here, they were sent east to Sackets Harbor to equip the American shipbuilding program.

During the first years of the war, the British avoided an attack on the fort, believing its defenses were too formidable to penetrate. In early May 1814, however, their chance came. The commander of the fort, Lt. Col. George Mitchell, had fewer than 300 men at his disposal and insufficient artillery to mount a defense.

The British arrived at Oswego on May 5. A storm over the lake prevented an attack that day—allowing the Americans to reposition artillery and move some supplies inland—but the following morning about 1,150 British troops landed near the American shore. The troops began their march through deep water, which ruined most of their ammunition and forced them to rely on their bayonets and the protective gunfire from Commodore James Lucas Yeo's ships. They faced a U.S. force of just 467 soldiers, many of whom were

inside the fort. Those manning the batteries fired at the British, killing or wounding many of them. However, the Americans could not defend against such a large force and retreated to Oswego Falls, first scuttling the schooner *Growler* and burning bridges.

The British captured the fort and the village. They commandeered some small schooners, seven cannon destined for Commodore Chauncey's fleet, and hundreds of barrels of supplies before burning the barracks and spiking the guns. On May 7 they withdrew to the lake and mounted a blockade. However, the battle only succeeded in delaying Chauncey's command of the lake.

**Visiting the fort** The star-shaped Fort Ontario that you see today is a U.S. structure, built in the 1840s. The site retains remnants of older buildings, including parts of the 1759 **earthworks** and **walls.** The interior of the fort portrays military life in the 1860s, with exhibits, battle reenactments, and tours of the **officers' quarters, barracks, powder magazine, guardhouse,** and a **storehouse**.

To imagine the British attack in 1812, sightseers can walk along the **ramparts** and look out over Lake Ontario where Yeo's ships once sailed. ∎

1 East Fourth St., Oswego, NY • 315-343-4711 • www.nysparks.com/historic-sites • $ • Closed mid-Oct. to mid-May

*Quick History*

**D**uring the British siege of Fort Ontario, the Americans defiantly nailed their flag to the flagpole. They continued to defend the flag as the British advanced on the fort, wounding British Lt. John Hewett of the Royal Marines three times as he ripped the flag from the pole. The flag dropped to the ground and the Americans retreated. Today, the captured flag is displayed in Scotland, in the ancestral home of British Gen. Gordon Drummond.

## » *Other Sites & Plaques*

### ✤ *Bridge Island/Chimney Island*
In early 1814 the British constructed a blockhouse and circular battery on Chimney Island (then Bridge Island) on the St. Lawrence River. Convoys and troops ferrying supplies along the river used the island as a protected rest stop. A plaque detailing the island's history stands near the shore on the mainland opposite. **Thousand Islands Parkway, east of Mallorytown Rd., Mallorytown Landing, ON**

### ★ *Brown Mansion*
American Brig. Gen. Jacob Brown of the New York militia, responsible for organizing U.S. defenses in the region and for the defeat of British forces at Sackets Harbor, built this limestone house between 1811 and 1815. The building now houses Brownville's public library. **216 Brown Blvd., Brownville, NY**

### ✤ *The Escape of the Royal George*
A plaque describes the naval chase of H.M.S *Royal George* by the U.S. fleet led by Commodore Isaac Chauncey (see p. 63). **Hwy. 33, west of Hwy. 21, near Greater Napanee, ON**

### ✤ *Kingston Navy Yard National Historic Site*
Kingston's Royal Navy Dockyard on Point Frederick was the only British naval base on Lake Ontario and the site of its wartime shipbuilding industry. There is a plaque dedicated to the yard, which closed in 1853, outside the Stone Frigate near the Royal Military College. **Royal Military College, Parade Sq., Point Frederick, Kingston, ON • www.parkscanada.gc.ca**

### ✤ *Raid on Elizabethtown*
On February 6, 1813, U.S. Captain Benjamin Forsyth, who led the successful raid on Gananoque, launched another surprise attack across the St. Lawrence River. Under cover of darkness, he led a force of around 200 men to the small village of Elizabethtown (now Brockville). He returned with muskets, prisoners, and rescued U.S. troops. A plaque entitled Forsyth's Raid 1813, at the end of Apple Street, south of Water Street West, details the attack. **Apple St., Brockville, ON • www.heritagetrust.on.ca**

### ✤ *Raid on Gananoque*
On September 21, 1812, Capt. Benjamin Forsyth conducted the first U.S. raid to take place along the St. Lawrence north shore. A stone monument on Gananoque's Stone Street South details the town's importance during the war, while a plaque on King Street, near the bridge, is dedicated to the raid. **Gananoque, ON • www.parkscanada.gc.ca**

### ★ *Sackets Harbor Military Cemetery*
Some 1812 officers are buried at this military cemetery, including Gen. Zebulon Pike, who died at the Battle of York in 1813. Most 1812 burials are in a marked mass grave in the former Madison Barracks. **Dodge Ave., Sackets Harbor, NY**

### ★ *Seaway Trail Discovery Center*
The trail links historic sites and remembrance gardens related to the War of 1812. Located in Sackets Harbor's historic Union Hotel, the Discovery Center provides a wealth of information about the trail and includes its own 1812 exhibit. **401 West Main St., Sackets Harbor, NY • www.seawaytrail.com/discoverycenter**

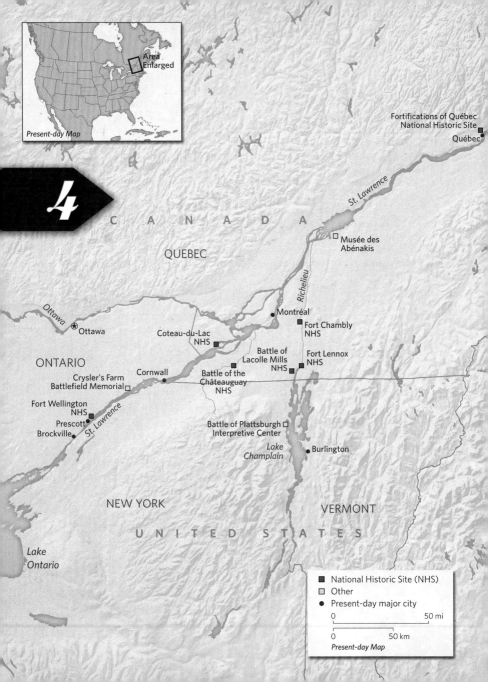

Fortifications of Québec
National Historic Site

Québec

**4**

C A N A D A

QUEBEC

Musée des
Abénakis

Richelieu

Ottawa

⊛ Ottawa

Montréal

Coteau-du-Lac
NHS

Fort Chambly
NHS

ONTARIO

Cornwall

Battle of
Lacolle Mills
NHS

Fort Lennox
NHS

Crysler's Farm
Battlefield Memorial

Battle of the
Châteauguay
NHS

Fort Wellington
NHS

St. Lawrence

Prescott

Brockville

Battle of Plattsburgh
Interpretive Center

Lake
Champlain

Burlington

NEW YORK

VERMONT

U N I T E D    S T A T E S

Lake
Ontario

■ National Historic Site (NHS)
□ Other
● Present-day major city

0 ——————— 50 mi

0 ——————— 50 km

*Present-day Map*

Present-day Map

Area
Enlarged

# St. Lawrence, Lake Champlain, & Richelieu Valley

At the start of the war, the Americans realized that if they could capture Montreal and occupy the St. Lawrence Valley, they could sever the flow of British troops and supplies to the Great Lakes. They hoped to achieve this by invading via Lake Champlain and the Richelieu Valley of southern Quebec, but mounted poorly organized invasion attempts in the first two years of the war. After the failed campaign of 1813, they did not mount a major invasion of Lower Canada again. In 1814, when Britain gained the upper hand in Europe, they planned aggressive counter-invasions of the U.S., but the tables had turned and their northern strategy collapsed with Master Commandant Thomas Macdonough's victory at the Battle of Plattsburgh in fall 1814.

**4**

Cannon from Fort Lennox on Île aux Noix in the Richelieu River

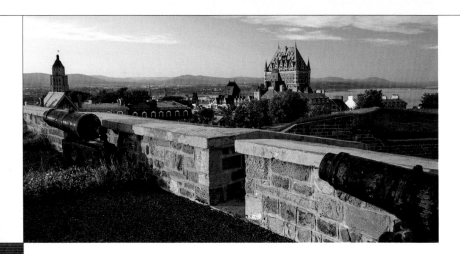

## ›› Fortifications of Québec National Historic Site

When the War of 1812 broke out, Quebec was the major fortification in British North America, serving as both the headquarters of the British Army and the seat of government. With easy access to the Atlantic Ocean and St. Lawrence Valley, the city was well placed to assist troop movements from Europe to Upper Canada, where most of the fighting took place. And its ring of walls and bastions protected it against attack from both the St. Lawrence River and the Plains of Abraham, a plateau to the west of the city.

Today's fortifications feature distinct areas: **Dufferin Terrace,** the **Governors' Walkway,** and **Montmorency Park** are perched along the bluffs, offering sweeping views over the river and the St. Lawrence Valley. At the Parks Canada kiosk on Dufferin Terrace, visitors can join a guided walk around the ramparts (mid-May to Oct.) or pick up a map. Partway round, on the east side of the Château Frontenac hotel, a deep

The fortifications provide a good view of Quebec's landmark Château Frontenac hotel, built in the late 19th century.

hole in the terrace provides a good view of the excavated ruins of the **Saint-Louis Forts** and **Châteaux.** Major archaeological digs in 2005 and 2007 revealed the remains of four forts built one on top of another, as well as 500,000 historical artifacts from the time of the French and British regimes. Among the many items on display in the **archaeological crypt** beneath the terrace are French, Dutch, and British china and glass, pipes, Papal insignia, and Native tools, pipes, beads, and coins. Tickets to the archaeological site are available at the kiosk on Dufferin Terrace.

**Artillery Park Heritage Site** on the west side of the old town encompasses several historic buildings, including the 18th-century Dauphine Redoubt, officers' quarters dating from just after the War of 1812, and an early 20th-century arsenal foundry. The **interpretive center** in the old foundry has exhibits on the French and British governors who ruled from Quebec, as well as the construction of the fortifications. Tours in French and English are led by guides clad in colonial-era dress. Reenactors demonstrate flintlock musket firing and cannon drills twice a day in July and August.

2 D'Auteuil St., Quebec City, QC • 418-648-7016 • www.parkscanada.gc.ca • $

## ›› COTEAU-DU-LAC NATIONAL HISTORIC SITE

Situated 24 miles (39 km) south of Montreal on the western bank of the St. Lawrence River, Coteau-du-Lac's importance lay in its canal lock (the first in North America), serving a canal that skirted rapids on the river at this point. The canal was a primitive forerunner of the St. Lawrence Seaway. Dug between 1779 and 1781, the lock was widened during the War of 1812 to expedite passage of the flat-bottomed barges known as "bateaux" taking supplies upriver to the Great Lakes region.

Concurrent with construction of the canal, the British built fortifications on the strip of land between the canal and the river to protect the river traffic that was vital to the development of Upper Canada. During the war, they bolstered their defenses along the canal and stationed a garrison of 60–80 men at Coteau-du-Lac.

Today, the site has a reproduction of a War of 1812 **blockhouse** and outdoor **gun platforms,** the original clover-shaped **earthwork battery,** and some brickwork

**A Coteau-du-Lac National Historic Site staff member represents a private in the Royal Artillery circa 1812. In the background is the reconstructed blockhouse.**

marking the position of the original **lock.** The park **visitor center** highlights the construction and history of the canal and the fort. Interpretive activities include a guided tour of the octagonal blockhouse, a cannon demonstration, a GPS treasure hunt, and hands-on encounters with the artifacts discovered at Coteau-du-Lac. Visitors can also follow a short interpretive trail taking in the fortifications, canal, archaeological sites, and the river.

308A Chemin du Fleuve, Coteau-du-Lac, QC • 450-763-5631 • www.parkscanada.ca • $ • **Closed early Sept. to late May**

## » BATTLE OF LACOLLE MILLS NATIONAL HISTORIC SITE

Built by the British to guard the western flank of the Richelieu River just above the border between Quebec Province and New York State, this blockhouse protected one of the main invasion routes into the St. Lawrence Valley. American forces attacked the blockhouse, a two-story wooden structure, and the stronger, nearby mill twice during the war, and both times the garrison succeeded in repelling them.

The first Battle of Lacolle Mills took place on November 20, 1812, when a large American force under Maj. Gen. Henry Dearborn (a veteran of the Revolutionary War) crossed into southern Quebec intent on establishing a forward base on British North American soil. Driving away a small garrison of British troops, Canadian volunteers, and Mohawk allies, Dearborn's men temporarily captured the blockhouse. But shortly afterward, American militia attacked the post and exchanged "friendly fire" with Dearborn's regulars. In the confusion, the Canadian commander Charles-Michel de Salaberry retook the bastion and the Americans retreated back across the border.

American forces mounted another attack on the mill on March 30, 1814, when Maj. Gen. James Wilkinson led an army of 4,000 troops down the Richelieu Valley. Even though British forces (estimated at around 80 men) under Maj. Richard Handcock were greatly outnumbered, mud and snow slowed the American attack enough for some 400 Canadian reinforcements to arrive by foot and river. By evening, Wilkinson had given up the fight and withdrawn his army back across the border.

The restored wooden **blockhouse** is open to the public, the only structure of its type remaining in Quebec province. Period furnishings and war mementos decorate the interior, while the facade is still scarred by musket holes from the twin battles. Guided talks are given in French and English. ∎

**1 Principale (Rte. 223), Saint-Paul-de-l'Île-aux-Noix, QC • 450-246-3227 • www .ileauxnoix.com • Closed Oct. to April**

**The modest two-story blockhouse at Lacolle Mills repelled two U.S. attacks.**

## >> BATTLE OF THE CHÂTEAUGUAY NATIONAL HISTORIC SITE

By the summer of 1813, American military commanders were convinced they could win the war outright by seizing control of the St. Lawrence River and severing the vital British supply line into Upper Canada. They drew up plans for a two-pronged invasion that included an attack on Kingston on the northern shore of Lake Ontario and an assault on Montreal in the heart of the St. Lawrence Valley. Maj. Gen. Wade Hampton commanded the Montreal campaign and by late September was mustering his forces near Lake Champlain.

Anticipating an attack on Montreal, the British command ordered Lt. Col. Charles-Michel de Salaberry to prepare defenses. De Salaberry gathered a combined force of Canadian regulars, militiamen, and Kahnawake Mohawk warriors to launch a preemptive strike on Hampton's base at Châteauguay Four Corners in New York State. After a brief skirmish, de Salaberry made a tactical retreat back across the border, his troops felling trees as they went to slow any American advance along the rural cart roads.

Discovering an excellent place to make a stand near Allan's Corner, de Salaberry ordered his troops to dig trenches and erect timber "abatis," field defenses constructed from felled trees with sharpened ends facing the enemy. Defying conventional military wisdom, the Canadian commander split his force, stationing his main body of 300 men on the north bank of the Châteauguay River, the remainder in reserve or protecting the flank.

**Double Canadian victory** From the outset, indecisiveness and personal animosities among the senior American commanders hindered their campaign, which was slow to start. Coming upon the enemy defenses on October 25, Hampton also divided his force on both sides of the river, hoping to outflank the Canadians with a clandestine nighttime move along the south bank.

Thick woods and difficult terrain thwarted the secret maneuver, and by the following morning Hampton found himself with little choice other than to make a direct frontal assault on the north bank. Falling behind the abatis, the greatly outnumbered Canadians put up a spirited defense that held throughout the day.

### Nearby & Noteworthy

**✳ FORT SAINT-JEAN** In 1775, the British built Fort Saint-Jean at the upper end of the Chambly Rapids, on the site of two previous French forts, and used it as a base in the War of 1812. Nothing remains of the fort, but the site is now home to the Royal Military College. The fort museum offers exhibits on 350 years of fort history. **15 Jacques-Cartier North, Saint-Jean-sur-Richelieu, QC, www.musee dufortsaintjean.ca**

**De Salaberry inspires his men. Though produced in 1884, this engraving gives a good impression of the densely wooded terrain where the battle was fought.**

On the south bank, a Canadian bayonet charge against U.S. units failed when its leaders fell wounded. Canadian troops began retreating in disarray. But de Salaberry, in a move that was to turn the tide of the entire battle, ordered his north bank forces to fire across the river into the advancing Americans. The devastating enfilade routed the American troops.

By now the American high command had sent Hampton new orders. These were rather vague, but combined with the setback to his flanking attack, they convinced Hampton that continuation of the battle was pointless. He ordered a full withdrawal and several days later slipped back into New York State.

Two weeks later, the British trounced the other American invasion force at Crysler's Farm on the St. Lawrence River (see p. 84). The twin defeats convinced the U.S. high command to abandon plans to capture Montreal and the St. Lawrence Valley.

Overnight, Châteauguay became a beacon for Quebec pride—a battle in which a Canadian force that was predominantly French-Canadian outwitted and defeated American regulars. De Salaberry, however, was not so pleased: Senior officers arrived after the battle had begun but in time to take some of the credit for his victory.

**Displays and tours**
Located in pastoral farm country, the Battle of the Châteauguay National Historic Site relives the epic Canadian victory through displays, talks, and self-guided battlefield tours. The modern **Interpretive Center** highlights include original weapons and documents donated by the de Salaberry family, as well as period uniforms and a scale model of the battlefield in front of a glass-walled viewpoint that overlooks the river and banks where the clash took place. Outside the center, an obelisk erected in 1895 by the Canadian Parliament commemorates the battle. Those craving a more in-depth experience can hike or bike a 10-mile (16 km), signposted archaeotour that includes the site of the Canadian headquarters, American camp, field hospital, an entrenchment, and a reproduction abatis where the Canadian front line once stood. ■

**2371 Rivière Châteauguay, Saint-Malachie-d'Ormstown, QC • 450-829-2003 • www.parkscanada.ca • $ • Closed mid-Sept. to mid-June**

## Quick History

Charles-Michel de Salaberry (1778–1829) was born into a family with a long history of military service to the French king and the British colonial government of Canada. By the age of 14 he was in uniform, fighting for the British in the West Indies and the Napoleonic Wars in Europe. By 25 he had earned his first command. On the eve of the War of 1812, de Salaberry took charge of a new volunteer light infantry unit called the Canadian Voltigeurs. Rather than drill them like militia, de Salaberry trained the Voltigeurs like regular army recruits, instilling discipline and a sense of pride. He experienced little battlefield service after Châteauguay as the Americans did not contemplate another assault on Quebec. Yet de Salaberry had secured his place as a Canadian folk hero. Some compared him to the Spartan king Leonidas, who, like de Salaberry, had led a force of 300 against a vastly larger foe. After the war, de Salaberry served in various Quebec government positions and in the Legislature of Lower Canada.

## »FORT LENNOX NATIONAL HISTORIC SITE

The Île aux Noix, an island in the middle of the Richelieu River north of Lake Champlain, sits amid a natural pathway between Lake Champlain and the St. Lawrence Valley that for hundreds of years served as both a trade route and invasion corridor. With narrow channels on both sides and bluffs at the southern end, the island was easily defendable even without human modification, but stout military bastions made it nearly impregnable and the British used it to support their naval operations on Lake Champlain. After the War of 1812, the British constructed the present fort, Fort Lennox, at the island's southern end.

The French military recognized the strategic importance of Île aux Noix when they built the first fortifications on the island to repel British attacks during the French and Indian War (1756–1763). In turn, the British constructed a more substantial bastion to defend against a possible American invasion during the Revolutionary War. As war broke out again in 1812, the British realized that Île aux Noix and its fort were the key to military operations in present-day southern Quebec and upstate New York.

Not long after hostilities commenced, the British established a naval yard on Île aux Noix and strengthened the fortress to take advantage of the island's proximity to the entrance to Lake Champlain. This gave them a base close to the American border from where they could control navigation on the lake. They then set about developing a fleet that could match anything the Americans might dispatch down the Richelieu River. Quite sizable ships were constructed from local materials and launched from the island, including H.M.S. *Confiance* (see box p. 80). The island fortifications also served to

protect British positions farther downriver at St. Jean and Chambly.

Turned away twice in battles at nearby Lacolle Mills, the Americans never mounted a land attack against Île aux Noix during the war. But their freshwater navy was a different matter, a constant threat to both the fort and downstream Canadian communities. On the morning of June 3, 1813, a pair of American warships—U.S.S. *Growler* and U.S.S. *Eagle*—attacked three British gunboats near the northern outlet of Lake Champlain. The British vessels fled down the Richelieu and the American ships followed to a point close to Île aux Noix, where they were engaged by the gunboats and British troops positioned on the banks. Both of the American warships eventually surrendered. The British towed them to the island shipyard, where they repaired them and converted them to British use. This short but decisive skirmish gave the British control of both the Richelieu and Lake Champlain for nearly a year, during which they used their own shipping to

**The guardhouse (below) and the officers' quarters lie on Fort Lennox's northeast side, close to the fort entrance.**

destroy American bases and supplies around the lake.

The current fort on the site, Fort Lennox, arose between 1819 and 1829. A British garrison was stationed there until 1870, after which Canadian militia used it for training. By the early 1920s, its military days were over. The fort's fame briefly revived when it was used as a camp for German Jewish refugees during World War II.

**The fort today** Fort Lennox National Historic Site covers the entire island and can be reached by ferry from the visitor center in the village of Saint-Paul-de-l'Île-aux-Noix on the west bank of the river. Perched at the island's southern end, the fort is shaped like a five-pointed star and surrounded by a water-filled moat. Within the ramparts are six buildings arrayed around a grassy parade ground. The largest of these is the long, Palladian-style **barracks** with an imposing stone facade. The smaller **Officers' Quarters,** with a stone portico and many interior architectural details still intact, is just as impressive. Other buildings include a powder magazine, armory, quartermaster's store, and guardhouse near the front gate. A plaque on the wall of the south passage

## Quick History

A 36-gun frigate constructed in the Île aux Noix naval yard, H.M.S. *Confiance* is the largest ship ever to have sailed on Lake Champlain. Its launch took place just in time for the British invasion of northern New York in September 1814, becoming the flagship of Capt. George Downie, though not for long. During the naval Battle of Plattsburgh on September 11, Downie was killed during an engagement with U.S.S. *Saratoga*. With several other officers dead or wounded, the badly damaged *Confiance* surrendered later in the day. It was repaired and converted into a U.S. warship, but never saw action again. It sank near the southern end of Lake Champlain in 1820. Retrieved from the lake bottom in the 1990s, its anchor now rests in front of Plattsburgh City Hall.

commemorates the role of officers and seamen who served in the Royal Navy and Provincial Marine on Lake Champlain and at the Battle of Plattsburgh (see box below).

Permanent exhibits include "The Gentlemen Officers," a display of uniforms, weapons, and everyday objects that disclose the life of British officers stationed on the island during the War of 1812 and later. "Fort Lennox: A Work by Royal Engineers" is a series of audio kiosks inside the North Magazine that describe the fort's construction.

Interpretive guides lead tours in French and English. Topics range from the general history of the island and fort, to 19th-century garrison life, food, military clothing, and equipment. Living history presentations take place on weekends.

During the summer, the fort stages special events, including after-dark lantern tours, family campouts on the parade ground, and a Fab Forts Weekend that includes "naval battles" with sponges, strategic "missions" for children, and a giant picnic on the parade ground. ∎

1 61st Ave., Saint-Paul-de-l'Île-aux-Noix, QC • 450-291-5700 • www.parkscanada.ca • $ • **Closed mid-Oct. to mid-May**

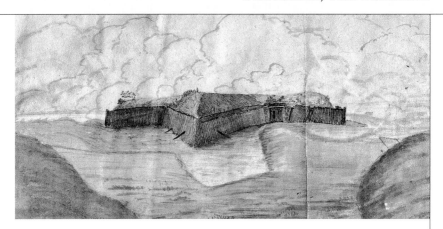

## » FORT WELLINGTON NATIONAL HISTORIC SITE

Perched on the north shore of the St. Lawrence River, the town of Prescott, Ontario, was an important transshipment point for people and cargo traveling on the river, and as soon as war broke out the British hurried to build fortifications there. In May 1813, they began the construction of Fort Wellington, named for the hero of Britain's Peninsular War against Napoleon. The fort was completed in late 1814, on the eve of peace. Although never attacked by U.S. forces during the war, it played a vital role in supporting the movement of British troops and supplies along the river.

Prescott was situated at the head of the Galop Rapids, a rocky hazard that impeded navigation on the St. Lawrence River between Montreal and Lake Ontario. Goods and people traveling upriver had to be portaged through the rapids in bateaux. At Prescott, they would transfer to larger ships for the journey on to the Great Lakes. The process was reversed for those traveling down the river. For the British, defense of the river passage here was essential to the conduct of the war in the Great Lakes region. And with New York State just across the river, the location was an obvious target for American attack.

The initial defenses, which the British created in 1812, included a wooden stockade built around a fortified house (now known as the Stockade Barracks, see box p. 83) in the town and earthworks mounted with a gun battery along the river. In 1813, the British decided that they needed a more substantial bastion and built a new fortress to the east

**Fort Wellington with the main gate on the right, as sketched in 1830**

of the town. By the war's end it had hefty wood-revetted earthwork ramparts. A one-story wooden blockhouse served as quarters for officers and enlisted men. Storage rooms, or casements, were built into the ramparts.

In February 1813, the British used the fort as the jumping-off point for a raid across the frozen St. Lawrence that captured Ogdensburg on the opposite shore and drove the U.S. military from the town for the rest of the war (see p. 66).

After the war, the British gradually reduced the garrison and finally abandoned the fort in 1833. They re-occupied and largely rebuilt Fort Wellington during the Upper Canadian Rebellion (1837–1838), an insurrection against British rule in the province, again to foil the possibility of an American invasion. The fort's active military career ended in 1869.

**Fort Wellington today** Although the ramparts and overall shape date from the War of 1812, today's Fort Wellington is more evocative of the 1840s, when the Royal Canadian Rifle Regiment was stationed there. The defenses include wooden **palisades** and 60-foot-thick (18 m) earthen **ramparts** with horizontal timber posts, known as "fraising,"

set just below the crest. A stone *caponnière,* a long, low building with openings that allow for flanking fire on enemy troops , projects from the southern wall. Visitors enter through the **original stone gate** into a large parade ground.

The most impressive building is the three-story **blockhouse.** With thick walls, multiple gun ports, trap doors to allow defenders to fire down from the upper floor, and a roof padded with sand and logs, it was well protected. The interior is now outfitted with an armory, powder magazine, storehouse, and soldiers barracks. The third floor is given over to displays on Fort Wellington's history.

The three-room **officers' quarters** was used by the fort commander. It has small windows that could double as loopholes and

**During cannon drill at Fort Wellington one gunner rams home the cannonball while another blocks the touch-hole with his hand to prevent a premature detonation.**

elegant campaign furniture, designed to be easily transportable. The **latrine** has separate sections for officers, women and children, and enlisted men. Archaeological excavations beneath and around the latrine yielded numerous artifacts, including leather boots, toys, ceramics, and medicine containers.

The visitor center features an orientation video and exhibits that explain the fort's role in helping to protect the British supply line along the St. Lawrence River. Among the artifacts is the wreck of a War of 1812–era British **gunboat** raised from the St. Lawrence

in 1967. The museum also has a scale model of Fort Wellington from around 1812.

**Reliving the past** Interpretive guides in period costume lead **tours** (weekends only) and are stationed around the fort to explain architectural features and fort life. Living history events include musket and cannon firing, 19th-century cooking demonstrations, and games that would have been played by soldiers and children living at the fort. High points of the Wellington summer season include Canada Day (July 1) and the annual Prescott Loyalist Days Military Pageant in August, which includes parades, fireworks, and events for children. ■

**370 Vankoughnet St., Prescott, ON • 613-925-2896 • www.parkscanada.ca • $ • Closed mid-Oct. to mid-May**

## >> CRYSLER'S FARM BATTLEFIELD MEMORIAL

Determined to capture Montreal, the Americans sent two armies into the St. Lawrence Valley in the fall of 1813. The larger of these, an 8,000-strong force under Maj. Gen. James Wilkinson, gathered at Sackets Harbor on Lake Ontario and started downriver from the Thousand Islands region in whatever boats they could muster. Despite foul weather and harassment from British gunboats and land-based militia, the Americans slowly but surely advanced.

It took Lt. Col. Joseph Wanton Morrison's Corps of Observation more than a fortnight to catch up with the Americans, who were camped on the Canadian shore near the top of the Long Sault Rapids. On the night of November 10, Morrison's force, which also included Mohawks from Tyendinaga and Kahnawake, camped 2 miles (3 km) upstream near Crysler's Farm, an area of muddy wheat fields, gullies, and marshy woodland that would favor his much smaller army, outnumbered three to one by the American force.

On the morning of November 11, with British gunboats bombarding his flotilla, Wilkinson dispatched Brig. Gen. John Boyd to attack Morrison's troops and quash the British threat. Struggling against the difficult terrain and highly trained redcoat regulars, Boyd's forces withdrew. By

mid-afternoon, the Americans were in retreat by boat and on foot. What remained of the American army made it through the Long Sault and landed near Cornwall, Ontario. On learning that American reinforcements would not be joining his beleaguered force, Wilkinson broke off his invasion of Lower Canada and retreated back to New York State.

Although Crysler's Farm was later designated as a national historic site, it disappeared beneath the St. Lawrence Seaway in the late 1950s.

Flanked by British and Canadian flags, a white granite **monument** honoring those who fought in the battle now overlooks the water in Crysler Park near Morrisburg. Housed in a building near the obelisk is a large mural depicting action from the battle.

**Upper Canada Village Rd., Morrisburg, ON • www.cryslersfarm.com**

**A memorial plaque giving a brief account of the battle stands near the obelisk in Crysler Park.**

### BATTLE OF CRYSLER'S FARM 1813

In November, 1813, an American army of some 8000 men, commanded by Major-General James Wilkinson, moved down the St. Lawrence en route to Montreal. Wilkinson was followed and harassed by a British corps of observation consisting of about 800 regulars, militia and Indians commanded by Lieut-Col Joseph Morrison. On November 11, Morrison's force, established in a defensive position on John Crysler's farm, was attacked by a contingent of the American army numbering about 4000 men commanded by Brigadier-General J.P. Boyd. The hard fought engagement ended with the Americans' withdrawal from the battlefield. This reverse, combined with the defeat of another invading army at Chateauguay on October 26, saved Canada from conquest in 1813.

Archaeological and Historic Sites Board of Ontario

## »FORT CHAMBLY NATIONAL HISTORIC SITE

In the 17th century, the French built the original Fort Chambly, 17 miles (27 km) due east of Montreal, to protect the city from a British attack. Taken by British forces in 1760 and captured by U.S. troops in 1775, the fort was back under British control by the outbreak of the War of 1812, one of a string of forts along the Richelieu River that protected Montreal and the St. Lawrence Valley from an American invasion. During the war the British developed a large military complex here by adding a number of new buildings outside the main fortification so that they could use it as a major staging ground for troops and supplies.

In 1665, French commander Jacques de Chambly and the Carignan-Salières Regiment constructed a large wooden stockade called Fort Saint-Louis at the foot of the Richelieu Rapids. The French launched raids against the Haudenosaunee from this fort, and some of their troops later returned to settle nearby. With the start of Queen Anne's War in 1701, the governor of New France decided to upgrade the stronghold to a larger stone fort able to ward off British invasion attempts.

Completed in 1711, Fort Chambly took a very similar form to what visitors see today. Its designer was Josué Dubois Berthelot de

**The dominating position of Fort Chambly overlooks the Chambly rapids, a narrow and turbulent section of the Richelieu River.**

Beaucours, a future governor of Montreal. The square design seems simple at first glance, but closer inspection reveals details that made Chambly military architecture appropriate for the time. Triangular bastions at the corners eliminated blind spots and expedited flanking fire during an assault on the walls. Gun ports were spread over several levels to amplify the firepower that could be brought to bear on the enemy. The design also features bartizans (wall turrets) and a few machicolations (openings in the walls through which the fort's defenders could shoot downward at attackers).

**British occupation** After seizing Canada from the French in 1760, the British military occupied the fort. They made few changes until 1812, when war broke out with the United States. The British chose Chambly as the major staging point for soldiers and supplies in the St. Lawrence theater.

At the height of the war, as many as 6,000 troops were stationed at Chambly awaiting deployment wherever they were needed. The base expanded to include around 40 buildings just east of the fort, including headquarters, hospital, barracks, magazines, and stables. The guardhouse built at this period still survives at the edge of the Fort Chambly site.

After the war, the fort gradually lost its strategic importance and the British finally closed it in 1860, selling off or dismantling many of the buildings. In spring 1861, the northern wall of the fort collapsed into the Richelieu River. But local journalist and historian Joseph-Octave Dion led a campaign to save the old stone fort, after which he himself lived at the fort as its guardian for 30 years, until his death in 1916.

**The restored fort** Set along the shore of an artificial lake called the Chambly Basin, this national historic site includes the fort and nearby parkland with a picnic area. It also

---

## Nearby & Noteworthy

**✳ LA MAISON DU COMMANDANT** The garrison commander and the officer in charge of artillery occupied this waterfront stone-and-shingle house, constructed in 1814, during the last year of the war. It is now a private home. An interpretive board outside describes the structure's history. *14 rue de Richelieu, Chambly, QC, www.ville.chambly.qc.ca*

**✳ DE SALABERRY HOUSE** French-Canadian war hero Charles-Michel de Salaberry built this three-story stone house near Fort Chambly right after the War of 1812 and lived there until his death in 1829. A plaque outside the residence (now a private home) describes the structure and its illustrious owner, who masterminded the Anglo-Canadian victory in the Battle of the Châteauguay. *18 rue de Richelieu, Chambly, QC, www.historicplaces.ca*

takes in a cemetery with graves from both the French and British periods, including Americans who fell in the Revolutionary War. Interpretive panels near the picnic area describe the fort's engineering and history. Permanent exhibits inside the fort use artifacts, videos, audio clips, models, and 3-D re-creations to show how the fort evolved over its 200 years of military service and what it was like being stationed there during French and British rule. They also include displays on fort benefactor Joseph-Octave Dion.

Fort Chambly offers a wide variety of living history and interpretation activities, from musket firing demonstrations to hands-on archaeological talks. (Archaeologists conducted unusually comprehensive major digs around the whole site during the 1970s.) One of the more popular is a program that offers visitors an opportunity to don reproduction uniforms of the 1665 Carignan-Salières Regiment and the 1750 Compagnie Franche de la Marine, two French units that occupied the fort in colonial times.

Like many 1812-era forts, Chambly stages reenactments and encampments during the summer season. The fort also holds a beer fest—focused on the history of brewing in New France and Lower Canada—in early September. And it reopens in late October on a single night before Halloween for a spooky, after-dark family event. ∎

**2 rue de Richelieu, Chambly, QC • 450-658-1585 • www.parkscanada.ca • $ • Closed mid-Oct. to early April**

**Reenactors on parade outside the walls of Fort Chambly wear the uniforms of Canadian Voltigeurs, a light infantry unit that mustered at the fort during the war.**

## » BATTLE OF PLATTSBURGH INTERPRETIVE CENTER

Wedged between Vermont and New York, and extending into southern Quebec, Lake Champlain was a strategic corridor for centuries. When the War of 1812 broke out, the British and Americans marshaled forces here. Armies and militia were mustered, small navies built, and raids undertaken from the start of the war until the final engagement in the region: the Battle of Plattsburgh.

On August 31, 1814, Lt. Gen. Sir George Prévost marched an 11,000-strong army made up of veterans of the Napoleonic Wars into New York. The British intended to gain control of the Champlain Valley for leverage in the anticipated treaty negotiations. Days earlier, the Secretary of War ordered the commander at Plattsburgh to march most of his 5,500 troops westward. This significant misjudgment left the remaining commander, Brig. Gen. Alexander Macomb, with 1,500 soldiers—most of whom were invalids or raw recruits—to defend Plattsburgh.

These remaining troops were reinforced, however, through an extraordinary response from volunteer militia units from Vermont, a state that had largely opposed the conflict. Many Vermonters had supplied British forces during the war—the main reason Prévost led his army down the western shore of the lake.

The British invasion was supported by a flotilla of Royal Navy ships commanded by Capt. George Downie. On September 11, 1814, Downie's ships rounded Cumberland Head to face a squadron commanded by Master Commandant Thomas Macdonough. Though almost evenly matched, the less-experienced Americans won the six-hour battle. The British defeat on the lake caused Prévost to retreat back into Lower Canada.

As part of a museum campus that overlooks Lake Champlain, the Battle of Plattsburgh Interpretive Center examines the causes of the war, the Champlain Valley's role in the conflict, and the war's impact on the local civilian population. ■

**31 Washington Rd., Plattsburgh, NY 12903 • 518-566-1814 • www.battleofplattsburgh.org • Groups $ • Closed Sun. to Tues.**

**In Julian Davidson's painting, "The Battle of Lake Champlain" (1884), U.S.S. *Eagle* and *Saratoga* fire on a stricken H.M.S. *Confiance*.**

## ›› OTHER SITES

✤ *MUSÉE DES ABÉNAKIS* Located on Abenakis of Odanak Territory, this museum tells the story of the Abenakis, an Algonquin-speaking tribe that occupied part of the St. Lawrence Valley during the War of 1812. Some tribe members supported the British during the war but most remained neutral. **108 Waban Aki St., Odanak, QC • 450-568-2600 • www.museedesabenakis.ca**

★ *BATTERY PARK* With a wonderful view of Lake Champlain, the park is named for an artillery battery that occupied the site during the War of 1812. The gunners repelled an attack on Burlington by a British fleet in August 1813. It was also the site of a military encampment and a hospital. **Battery St., Burlington, VT • 802-864-0123 • www.enjoyburlington.com**

★ *LAKE CHAMPLAIN MARITIME MUSEUM* Among the museum's War of 1812 artifacts are anchors and stoneware from warships that participated in the Battle of Plattsburgh, as well as musket balls, powder measures, and ax heads recovered from the Poultney River, where the U.S. fleet was abandoned after the war. During the season, the museum offers lectures and guided gig and canoe tours on the lakeshore. **4472 Basin Harbor Rd., Vergennes, VT • 802-475-2022 • www.lcmm.org**

✤ *CATHEDRAL OF THE HOLY TRINITY* Modeled after St. Martin-in-the-Fields Church in London, England, and consecrated in 1804, Holy Trinity was one of Canada's first Palladian-style structures. Designed by two Royal Artillery officers,

Holy Trinity served as the home church of the British high command inside the walls of Quebec City during the War of 1812. **31 rue des Jardins, Quebec City, QC • 418-692-2193 • www.cathedral.ca**

★ *KENT-DELORD HOUSE* One of 11 sites featured on the Champlain Valley National Heritage Partnership's War of 1812 Interpretive Trail, Kent-Delord House became Plattsburgh's social nexus during the war years, and British officers used it as their headquarters during the 1814 Battle of Plattsburgh. Throughout the war, owner Henry Delord sold a range of goods to American troops (often on credit). Today, the house contains a large collection of furniture and possessions that belonged to the Delord family and subsequent occupants, including early 19th-century furnishings, family portraits, and personal effects. Events at the house include specialized tours and living history presentations. **17 Cumberland Ave., Plattsburgh, NY • 518-561-1035 • www.kentdelordhouse.org**

★ *PLATTSBURGH CITY HALL AND MACDONOUGH MONUMENT* Celebrated American architect John Russell Pope designed both Plattsburgh City Hall and the Battle of Plattsburgh monument across the street. Surmounted by a bronze eagle, the 135-foot (40 m) limestone obelisk commemorates the American victory on Lake Champlain and U.S. commander Thomas Macdonough. Stone friezes around the base honor four of his warships—*Saratoga, Ticonderoga, Eagle,* and *Preble.* The anchor of the British flagship H.M.S. *Confiance* is on display in the city hall's main lobby. **41 City Hall Pl., Plattsburgh, NY • 518-563-7701 • www.cityofplattsburgh.com**

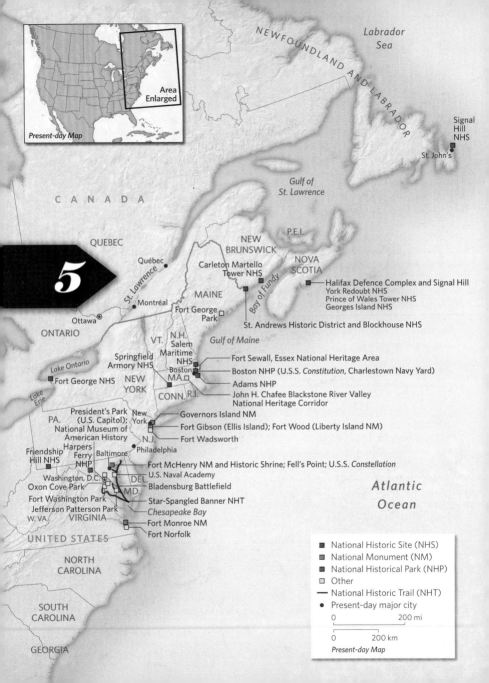

Labrador Sea

NEWFOUNDLAND AND LABRADOR

Signal Hill NHS

St. John's

Gulf of St. Lawrence

CANADA

QUEBEC

Québec

**5**

St. Lawrence

Montréal

Ottawa

ONTARIO

NEW BRUNSWICK

P.E.I.

NOVA SCOTIA

Carleton Martello Tower NHS

MAINE

Bay of Fundy

Fort George Park

Halifax Defence Complex and Signal Hill
York Redoubt NHS
Prince of Wales Tower NHS
Georges Island NHS

St. Andrews Historic District and Blockhouse NHS

VT.   N.H.
Salem Maritime NHS

Gulf of Maine

Springfield Armory NHS

Lake Ontario

Fort George NHS

NEW YORK

Boston
MA.

Fort Sewall, Essex National Heritage Area

Boston NHP (U.S.S. *Constitution*, Charlestown Navy Yard)

Adams NHP

Lake Erie

CONN.   R.I.

John H. Chafee Blackstone River Valley National Heritage Corridor

PA.

President's Park (U.S. Capitol);
National Museum of American History

New York

Governors Island NM

Fort Gibson (Ellis Island); Fort Wood (Liberty Island NM)

Fort Wadsworth

Friendship Hill NHS

Harpers Ferry NHP

Baltimore

N.J.

Philadelphia

Washington, D.C.

DEL.

Fort McHenry NM and Historic Shrine; Fell's Point; U.S.S. *Constellation*

U.S. Naval Academy

Oxon Cove Park

MD.

Bladensburg Battlefield

Fort Washington Park

Jefferson Patterson Park

Star-Spangled Banner NHT

W. VA.   VIRGINIA

*Chesapeake Bay*

Fort Monroe NM

Fort Norfolk

UNITED STATES

*Atlantic Ocean*

NORTH CAROLINA

SOUTH CAROLINA

GEORGIA

■ National Historic Site (NHS)
■ National Monument (NM)
■ National Historical Park (NHP)
□ Other
— National Historic Trail (NHT)
● Present-day major city

0          200 mi
0          200 km

*Present-day Map*

Area Enlarged

*Present-day Map*

# ATLANTIC SEABOARD, ATLANTIC CANADA, & THE CHESAPEAKE

The Atlantic coast was a key battleground in the War of 1812. Britain, the world's leading naval power at the time, blockaded much of the coast, while the U.S. Navy was well-trained and expanding. Both countries boosted their naval capacity by employing privateers. The end of the Napoleonic Wars in Europe in April 1814 enabled Britain to transfer ships to America. Thus reinforced, the British captured Washington, D.C., in August 1814, but their attack on Baltimore in September failed, and they never penetrated the defenses around New York.

5

*Friendship of Salem,*
Salem Maritime NHS

## ›› ST. ANDREWS HISTORIC DISTRICT AND BLOCKHOUSE

In 1783, Loyalists to the British crown who had moved north after the Revolutionary War founded the town of St. Andrews on an inlet in New Brunswick's Bay of Fundy. The town's **Historic District** is a rare surviving example of British colonial town planning. It retains its original gridiron plan and is ringed by common land. Many 18th- and 19th-century buildings survive, including some that were constructed in Castine, Maine, across the border, and then dismantled and brought to St. Andrews by barge by the settlers.

St. Andrews played a modest role in the War of 1812 as a base for British privateers and troops. However, its residents feared attack from American

St. Andrews blockhouse faces the bay as though still expecting attack.

privateers and raised money to construct two batteries of cannon to defend the town. These were the only privately funded defenses in Canada during the war. Capt. James McLaughlin ordered the addition of a third. Protecting each battery was a wooden blockhouse, a small defensive structure from which soldiers could fire at enemy troops. Completed in 1813, these blockhouses never faced attack.

The one surviving **blockhouse,** at the west end of town, overlooking the harbor, is the second-oldest blockhouse in Canada (the oldest is at Fort Edward in Nova Scotia). Its interior is furnished as it might have been during the

### Quick History

**B**lockhouses were small isolated forts, usually in the form of a single building. They were typically made of wood and had two or three stories with loopholes and gun ports through which defenders could fire upon attackers. Due to their simple design and an abundance of timber, they served as defensive strong points in frontier areas throughout North America.

War of 1812. Outside the blockhouse stand three 18-pound cannon dating from the mid-18th century.

**St. Andrews Historic District, St. Andrews, NB • 506-529-3556 • www.parkscanada.gc.ca; Blockhouse, 23 Joes Point Rd., St. Andrews, NB • 506-529-4270 • www.parkscanada.gc.ca • Closed Sept. to May**

## ›› CARLETON MARTELLO TOWER NATIONAL HISTORIC SITE

Saint John is the largest settlement in New Brunswick and was Canada's first incorporated city. Situated at the mouth of the Saint John River, it occupies a vital strategic position on the landward route into the interior of Canada. For this reason, the British reinforced its defenses when fighting broke out in 1812.

In 1813, they began building a martello tower to defend the western approaches to the town. Circular forts with thick stone walls and accessible by a door in the upper story (barracks floor), martello towers housed both cannon and soldiers. Between 1810 and 1847, at least 11 such towers were built along the coast of Canada. By the time the Carleton tower was completed in 1815, the War of 1812 had come to an end. The tower served as a barracks until the 1860s.

The tower's **visitor center** contains an exhibition on the history of Saint John and its tower, including a short film explaining the role that the town played in the War of 1812. The **tower** contains a re-creation of the 19th-century **barracks.** A highlight is the **panoramic view** over Saint John and the Bay of Fundy from the tower's roof.

**454 Whipple St., Saint John, NB • 506-636-4011 • www.parkscanada.ca • $ • Closed early Oct. to May**

## »Halifax Defence Complex and Signal Hill

The Maritime Provinces played an important role in the defense of Canada in the War of 1812. In Nova Scotia, Halifax, with its deep harbor, was the headquarters of the British Royal Navy's North Atlantic Squadron and protected by an elaborate defensive system. Today, five of the forts and batteries constructed by the British are national historic sites known collectively as the Halifax Defence Complex. In Newfoundland and Labrador, the city of St. John's was equally well-defended: Fortifications on Signal Hill, built during the 18th-century wars against the French, guarded the Narrows at the entrance to St. John's harbor.

**Halifax Citadel** Even though Halifax was the center of British naval operations in 1812, its Citadel, the third on the site, never had to defend it in earnest. Built between 1796 and 1800 by Prince Edward, Duke of Kent, and the first fort at Halifax to be sited directly on top of the hill, it formed part of a formidable wider defense system. It comprised a barracks, provision store, and powder magazine. After the War of 1812, the fortress fell into disrepair and was replaced in 1856 by a fourth fort, the star-shaped Citadel that you see today, built between 1828 and 1856.

The strategic value of Citadel Hill, which rises above the harbor, had long been appreciated. British forces built the first fort

### Quick History

Many of the military preparations for the War of 1812 were ordered by Prince Edward, Duke of Kent (1767–1820), including those at Halifax. The fourth son of George III, Edward served in British North America from 1791–1800, eventually becoming commander in chief of forces in the whole of British North America. After returning to Britain in 1802, he was appointed Governor of Gibraltar. He eventually married at the age of 50. His only child, a daughter, became Queen Victoria.

on the site in 1749. They had been sent to Nova Scotia to suppress a revolt by Acadian settlers and their Mi'kmag allies in what became known as Father Le Loutre's War. Lord Edward Cornwallis established a settlement here and constructed a stockade with an easily defensible location, 200 feet (60 m) above the harbor's western shore.

The panoramic view of the harbor remains one of the Citadel's enduring attractions. Visitors can tour the building from its **underground powder magazines** to the **barracks,** where they can try on a soldier's hat or attempt to lift a fully loaded kit bag. Volunteer reenactors dressed in 19th-century uniform patrol the parade ground. The skirl of bagpipes or the sound

With carefully choreographed movements, members of the Royal Artillery load the cannon with powder, push it into position, and fire it each day at noon at the Halifax Citadel.

of fife and drum accompanies the tread of marching feet. Since 1856, a **noon gun** fired from the Citadel has told the citizens of Halifax the correct time.

**5425 Sackville St., Halifax, NS • www .parkscanada.ca • $ • Closed Nov. to early May**

**Prince of Wales Tower National Historic Site** This mini fortress constructed in 1796–1797, also at the command of the Duke of Kent, was the first line of defense for Halifax harbor. The British built it to protect the batteries set up in 1793 along the shores of Point Pleasant to deter French landing parties.

The tower, almost three times as wide as it is high, is a typical martello tower. These squat, round, and extremely strong stone fortresses, named for a 16th-century tower at Martello (now Mortella) on the Mediterranean island of Corsica, sprang up around the coasts of Britain and its colonies during Britain's wars with Napoleonic France. In season, visitors can view the first floor, which was used for storage, and the **barracks** on the second floor, and climb on to the roof, where six guns would have pointed out to sea.

**Point Pleasant Park, Halifax, NS • www .parkscanada.ca • Interior closed Sept. to May**

**York Redoubt National Historic Site** On a promontory high above the entrance to Halifax harbor stands York Redoubt. The first gunners stationed here in 1793 would have watched all the comings and goings in the narrow strait and out toward the ocean. They would have made life uncomfortable for any enemy vessels entering the harbor.

The very presence of big guns here was a provocation to Britain's enemies, so Prince Edward, Duke of Kent, Britain's commander in chief, had the battery strengthened between 1795 and 1800. Further modifications continued well into the modern era. A World War II command post from which soldiers kept watch for German submarines remains. Interpretive panels tell the story of the site. Look out for the stone foundations of a **martello tower** dating from the War of 1812.

Purcells Cove Rd., Halifax, NS • 850-872-7208 • www.parkscanada.ca

**Georges Island National Historic Site**
Between the batteries here, in the middle of Halifax harbor, a few hundred yards

### Nearby & Noteworthy

✳ **Fort McNab** The fifth fort in the Halifax Defence Complex was built between 1888 and 1892 at the southern end of McNab Island to guard the outer channels of the harbor. It can be visited by ferry from the Halifax waterfront. *McNab Island, NS, www.parkscanada.ca*

Georges Island in Halifax harbor formed part of the Halifax Defence Complex. Fort Charlotte was built on the island by Price Edward, Duke of Kent, in 1793.

offshore, and those of Halifax Citadel (see pp. 94–95), the most vital anchorages could be kept under the closest possible protection. Even so, the island's defensive possibilities were not fully realized until 1793, when the Duke of Kent built a star-shaped stone fortress, which he named Fort Charlotte for his mother, the Queen. A martello tower, since destroyed, was added during the War of 1812.

Many of the ruined gun emplacements and barrack blocks were added after the war, when a new fort was built, but the central stronghold of Fort Charlotte, its walls and ditches, offer a sense of how the fort would have looked in 1812. The island is only open to the public for special events, but boat tours from Halifax waterfront pass close to the shore and offer good views.

**Georges Island, Halifax, NS • www.historic places.ca • Closed to the public**

**Signal Hill** Built at the turn of the 20th century, **Cabot Tower** on Signal Hill, Newfoundland and Labrador, is St. John's most visible landmark. It was near this site that Guglielmo Marconi's first transatlantic wireless signal was received. But Signal Hill acquired its name much earlier. In the Napoleonic era, it was used for signaling to ships offshore, using flags.

St. John's was one of Atlantic Canada's most crucial seaports. In the mid-18th century British and French forces fought for control of the area. In 1762, the two foes fought on the slopes of the hill.

The British continued to guard this area and the rich fishing grounds off the coast by building and reinforcing fortifications on Signal Hill. The War of 1812 changed little: The enemy may have been different but St. John's strategic value was the same.

From the summit, a moderately strenuous hike, parts of it on a wooden stairway, leads along the coastline, through the historic "battery" community, and all the way down to the center of St. John's, affording views of shipping entering the harbor, and even whales and icebergs depending on the season. In July and August, the **Signal Hill Tattoo**, takes place twice a day four times a week (Wednesday, Thursday, Saturday, and Sunday). Re-enactors perform military music and drill and in the uniform of the Grenadier Company, Royal Newfoundland Regiment of Foot. On alternate days, the 1812-era Royal Newfoundland Fencible Regiment, a company that saw action in all theaters of the War of 1812, also performs. ∎

**Signal Hill Rd., St. John's, NL • 709-772-5367 • www.parkscanada.ca • $ • Visitor Interpretation Centre closed mid-Oct. to mid-May; Cabot Tower closed mid-Nov. to mid-April**

## >> ADAMS NATIONAL HISTORICAL PARK

Two American presidents who influenced the War of 1812, John Adams and his son John Quincy Adams, were born and raised on the two properties comprising the Adams National Historical Park, 10 miles (16 km) south of Boston.

As Vice President (1789–1797) and President (1797–1801), John Adams was an advocate for a larger U.S. Navy. During his administration, the Navy launched six frigates that would later serve in the War of 1812 and win notable victories despite the overwhelming strength of the British. One of them, the U.S.S. *Constitution* (see p. 100), defeated five British warships.

### Nearby & Noteworthy

✶ **ABIGAIL ADAMS BIRTHPLACE** Abigail Smith Adams was born in a house near this site in 1744. This house, a restoration of that structure, contains furniture and objects from the mid-18th century. *180 Norton St., Weymouth, MA, www.abigailadamsbirthplace.com*

✶ **MASSACHUSETTS HISTORICAL SOCIETY** The state's historical treasure chest preserves war-related items including letters, broadsides, and a British cannon from the Battle of New Orleans. *1154 Boylston St., Boston, MA, www.masshist.org*

✶ **SCITUATE LIGHTHOUSE** Legend has it that two young daughters of lightkeeper Simeon Bates thwarted a British naval raid on Scituate in 1814 by playing their fife and drum to mimic the arrival of American militia. *100 Lighthouse Rd., Scituate, MA, www.lighthouse.cc/scituate*

✶ **UNITED FIRST PARISH CHURCH** This Greek Revival church is the burial place of both the Adams presidents and their wives. *1306 Hancock St., Quincy, MA, www.ufpc.org*

John Quincy Adams was serving as the U.S. Minister to Russia during the War of 1812, a war he believed was inevitable if the United States was to cast off the last shackles of colonial tyranny and become the dominant power in North America.

As the war was winding down in 1814, President James Madison asked John Quincy Adams to travel from Russia to Ghent in Belgium to negotiate the peace treaty. After signing the accord on Christmas Eve 1814, Adams remarked that he hoped the Treaty of Ghent would be "the last treaty of peace between Great Britain and the United States." And indeed it was.

The **Adams National Historical Park Visitor Center,** located inside the Galleria at President's Place in Quincy, is the starting point for guided tours of the two **presidential birthplaces** in south Quincy and the **Old House at Peacefield** where four generations of the Adams family lived. Tours last approximately two hours and are conducted by trolley.

**1250 Hancock St., Quincy, MA • 617-770-1175 • www.nps.gov/adam • $ • Closed mid-Nov. to mid-April**

## >> SALEM MARITIME NATIONAL HISTORIC SITE

Salem played a key role in the maritime history of the young United States. With a long history of shipbuilding and global trade, the Massachusetts port had vested interests in free trade and the impressment of American sailors—issues that helped spark the War of 1812 (see p. 12). Once war started, Salem became a base for American privateers—privately owned vessels sanctioned by the government to attack British shipping in the North Atlantic.

More than 40 privateers operated out of Salem during the War of 1812, including legendary ships like *Fame*, *Black Vomit*, and *Revenge*. The best ships were exceedingly fast, skippered by men who knew the local waters well, and owned by locals motivated by patriotic duty and the chance to make a profit. By the end of the war, privateers had taken more British ships than the U.S. Navy.

Salem's other contribution to the war effort was the U.S.S. *Essex*, a 32-gun frigate built by Salem shipbuilder Enos Briggs and launched in 1799. It was one of the Navy's fastest ships and famous for decimating the British whaling fleet in the South Atlantic and South Pacific until its capture by the British in March 1814.

Moored at the Derby Wharf on the waterfront is the *Friendship*, a copy of a 1797 East Indiaman merchant sailing vessel captured by a British warship in September 1812. Guided tours of the *Friendship* include a look at the main deck and the crew's quarters. There is also a regular program of hands-on events on themes such as navigation and cargo-handling during the late 18th century.

**193 Derby St., Salem, MA • 978-740-1650 • www.nps.gov/sama • $**

**The Old House at Peacefield was built in 1731. It is set in 18th-century-style formal gardens.**

## » *U.S.S.* Constitution *and* Charlestown Navy Yard (Boston NHP)

The victor of several naval encounters in the War of 1812, the U.S.S. *Constitution* was the most famous American ship of the time. Now a museum ship, it is moored in Charlestown Navy Yard, a supply and repair center during the War of 1812 and now part of Boston National Historical Park. Boston was an obvious choice for a naval yard—a narrow entrance to its harbor made it easy to defend—but the British blockade of the port during the war crippled the local economy. Several battles erupted in the waters off Boston, including a confrontation between H.M.S. *Shannon* and U.S.S. *Chesapeake* in June 1813.

**U.S.S. *Constitution*** Launched in 1797, the *Constitution* is the oldest commissioned warship in the world that is still afloat. A wooden, three-masted frigate, it won its nickname, "Old Ironsides," during a battle with the Royal Navy's H.M.S. *Guerriere* in August 1812. The two ships exchanged fire, but the British shot appeared to bounce off the *Constitution*'s thick wooden hull, causing

an American sailor to exclaim, "Huzza! Her sides are made of iron!" The *Constitution* disabled the British ship and burned it at sea. It went on to capture four more British ships and did much to raise American morale.

Taken out of active service in 1881, the *Constitution* opened to the public in the early 1900s. Now berthed in the Charlestown Navy Yard, it is crewed by members of the

**A painting of U.S.S. Constitution's victory over H.M.S. Guerriere in August 1812**

Navy, who conduct tours (every half hour). On July 4, the *Constitution*, under tug power, cruises Boston Harbor and fires a 21-gun salute to commemorate U.S. independence. Members of the public can apply to the Navy for tickets, which are allocated by lottery.

Close to the ship is the **U.S.S. Constitution Museum.** Exhibits include personal possessions of the ship's crew, documents, weapons, and spoils of war. A hands-on experience allows visitors to sample life aboard a 19th-century ship, including scrubbing the deck and crawling into a hammock.

U.S.S. *Constitution*, Building 5, Charlestown Navy Yard, Boston, MA • www.history.navy.mil/ussconstitution • closed Mon. to Wed. Nov. to Mar., Mon. April to Oct.; U.S.S. *Constitution* Museum, Building 22, Charlestown Navy Yard, Boston • 617-426-1812 • www.ussconstitutionmuseum.org

**Charlestown Navy Yard** Established in 1800 to build warships for the American Navy, the Charlestown Navy Yard was a center for the repair and supply of American Navy ships during the War of 1812.

## Quick History

Many other famous ships have been built in Charlestown. **U.S.S. *Independence*,** launched in 1814 to protect the waters around Boston, was the first "ship of the line" commissioned by the U.S. Navy. The frigate **U.S.S. *Merrimack*,** launched in Charlestown in 1855, was based in Virginia when the Civil War broke out in 1861. To prevent it from falling into Confederate hands, the U.S. Navy burned and sank it. The Confederacy then raised the wreck, covered it in iron, and renamed it the U.S.S. *Virginia*. In the 20th century, the destroyer **U.S.S. *Forrest*,** launched in 1941, served in both the Atlantic and the Pacific during World War II. It was named for Dulany Forrest, a lieutenant who served in the U.S. Navy during the War of 1812 and won renown during the Battle of Lake Erie (see p. 33).

In 1813, a famous battle between the U.S.S. *Chesapeake* and H.M.S. *Shannon* took place off Boston Light. Leaving Charlestown on June 1, the American ship sailed out to meet the *Shannon*. The two ships exchanged heavy fire, and the *Chesapeake*'s mortally wounded captain, James Lawrence, urged his crew, "Don't give up the ship!" Unable to follow his final order, the crew fled below deck and the American ship was boarded, captured, and taken to Halifax, Nova Scotia. It became part of the British Royal Navy and from then on sailed as H.M.S. *Chesapeake*.

The Charlestown Navy Yard closed as a shipyard in 1974, having built more than 200 warships and repaired thousands more. In addition to the *Constitution*, look out for **U.S.S. *Cassin Young*,** a steel destroyer from World War II, which is also open for tours. Although the *Cassin Young* was built in California, 14 similar vessels were built in this yard.

There are more than 20 historic buildings, as well as one of the first **dry docks** built in the U.S., dating from 1833. Charlestown's 30-acre (12 ha) historic area can be reached by water shuttle from other parts of the city. ∎

**Visitor Center, Building 5, Charlestown Navy Yard, Charlestown, MA • 617-242-5601 • www.nps.gov/bost**

## » Governors Island National Monument

Now open to the public after years as a military base, Governors Island is home to two of the more remarkable military structures on the mid-Atlantic coast—Castle Williams and Fort Jay. Situated at the confluence of the Hudson and East Rivers just 800 yards (730 m) from the tip of Manhattan, they were perfectly placed to protect the city. Although neither saw action during the War of 1812, they formed part of a network of fortifications designed to repel a British attack on New York.

Built between 1807 and 1811, **Castle Williams** is named for its chief engineer, Col. Jonathan Williams, the grandnephew of Benjamin Franklin. Williams used red limestone to create a circular structure (roundhouse) with a hundred guns spread over three tiers. As well as providing a 220-degree arc of fire, the curved walls were thought to be better than flat surfaces at repelling cannonballs.

In summer, you can take a guided tour of the fort's interior and parapet, with its spectacular views of New York Harbor, the Statue of Liberty, and Lower Manhattan. A short walk to the east of Castle Williams,

landlocked **Fort Jay** was built in 1797–1798 over an earthworks battery dating from the Revolutionary War. Colonel Williams reinforced it just before the War of 1812, adding brick and granite facades, a dry moat, and the five ravelins (triangular outworks). The Trophée d'Armes sculpture carved on the sally port (entry gate) in the 1790s is one of the oldest stone monuments in the U.S. Hewn from red sandstone, its design incorporates military and patriotic symbols including flags, weapons, and an eagle.

**Ferry from Battery Maritime Building, Slip 7, New York, NY • 212-825-3045 • www.nps.gov/gois • Closed Mon.,Tues. and Oct. to May. On Wed. to Fri. it can be visited on tours conducted by a park ranger; on weekends, Memorial Day, and Labor Day it can be visited independently.**

---

### Nearby & Noteworthy

❋ **BROOKLYN NAVY YARD** Designed by and named for inventor Robert Fulton, the catamaran steam frigate *Fulton* (also called the *Demologos*) was the first U.S. warship to be powered by steam. Built in 1814–1815, it was not launched in time to serve in the War of 1812. *63 Flushing Ave., Brooklyn, NY 11205, www.brooklynnavyyard.org*

❋ **CASTLE CLINTON** The west battery of the New York defense system, this sandstone fortress at the lower end of Manhattan complemented Castle William (the east battery). *Battery Park, New York, NY, www.nps.gov/cacl*

❋ **HORTON POINT.** In June 1814, British warships destroyed a U.S. "torpedo boat" that had run aground under the Horton Point bluffs off Long Island. This was one of the first battles involving a submarine in naval history. *Southold, Long Island, NY*

---

## » Fort Wood (Liberty Island) and Fort Gibson (Ellis Island)

It's hard to imagine New York Harbor without Lady Liberty. But such was the case before 1876, when engineers assembled the statue, created in Paris, on an island near the Jersey shore. In 1807, the U.S. military had built **Fort Wood** on the island, equipping it with 24 guns and storage for 200 barrels of gunpowder. In the War of 1812, while other cities on the eastern seaboard fell to the British, New York remained unscathed.

Ellis Island (foreground), the site of Fort Gibson, and Liberty Island (behind), the site of Fort Wood. The two forts formed part of an elaborate defensive system that successfully protected New York Harbor during the War of 1812.

Shaped like an 11-pointed star, the citadel was garrisoned with artillery and infantry troops. Originally called the Works on Bedloe's Island, it was renamed Fort Wood in memory of Eleazer D. Wood, an army engineer who was killed during the 1814 siege of Fort Erie. In the 1840s, the outer walls were faced with granite. Later still, it became the base of the Statue of Liberty.

Before it became America's most celebrated immigration gateway, nearby Ellis Island, then called Oyster Island, served as part of New York Harbor's defensive system during the War of 1812. **Fort Gibson,** built

in 1795, had a dozen embrasures for heavy guns, plus a magazine and an L-shaped barracks. During the war, it also served as a camp for British prisoners of war. The fort was named for Col. James Gibson of Delaware, who fell at Fort Erie.

All that can be seen of the fort today are its foundations, uncovered when the American Immigrant Wall of Honor was built. They are marked by a plaque. Both Fort Wood and Fort Gibson form part of the Statue of Liberty National Monument.

**Ferry from Battery Park Place, New York, NY, or Liberty State Park, 1 Audrey Zapp Dr., Jersey City, NJ • 212-363-3200 • www.nps.gov/stli • $**

## ›› HARPERS FERRY NATIONAL HISTORICAL PARK

In 1794, George Washington selected the town of Harpers Ferry, at the confluence of the Potomac and Shenandoah Rivers, as the site of a national armory. The rivers powered the machinery that made the weaponry and were used for shipping it westward. During the War of 1812, the armory produced 30,000 muskets and rifles for the U.S. Army.

The town supplied at least seven companies of volunteers for the U.S. Army in the war. John Butler, a free man of color from Harpers Ferry, served on the U.S.S. *United States* during its victory over H.M.S. *Macedonian*. **Williamson's Tavern,** now a park exhibit, served as a recruiting station.

Today, the park covers 3,700 acres (1,500 ha) of countryside in three states, with 20 miles (32 km) of hiking trails linking natural and historical highlights. The view of the rivers and mountains was described by Thomas Jefferson as "one of the most stupendous scenes in nature."

**171 Shoreline Dr., Harpers Ferry, WV • 304-535-6029 • www.nps.gov/hafe • $**

## ›› U.S. CAPITOL AND PRESIDENT'S HOUSE (THE WHITE HOUSE)

On August 24, 1814, British forces, led by Maj. Gen. Robert Ross, marched on Washington and torched the U.S. Capitol, the President's House, and other public buildings. American forces were unprepared for an attack, believing Washington had limited strategic importance for the British.

**Harpers Ferry Armory pictured in 1862, shortly before much of the armory was destroyed during the Civil War**

A storm stopped the fire from destroying the Capitol completely, but, in the words of its architect Benjamin Henry Latrobe, it was reduced to "a most magnificent ruin." After the war, Latrobe set about restoring the building, with Charles Bulfinch taking over the reins in 1818.

Both the Capitol and the White House (then called the President's House) are on the Star-Spangled Banner Trail (see p. 106). The **U.S. Capitol Visitor Center,** beneath the East Plaza of the Capitol, includes a model of Latrobe's plan to rebuild it as well as a letter from Thomas Jefferson offering to sell his own library to replace the congressional library lost in the fire.

**President's House** The British also torched the President's House, now known as the White House, and the home of every American President except George Washington. Only the south wall and the four-columned front of the north wall survived. The rest was rebuilt in 1817. A **visitor center** details the history of the building. Tours of the White House can be arranged by contacting your member of Congress or embassy. The self-guided 30-minute tour includes the **Library, East Room, Green, Blue** and **Red Rooms,** and the **State Dining Room.**

U.S. Capitol, East Capitol St., NE, and 1st St., Washington, DC • 202-226-8000 • www.visitthecapitol.gov; White House, 1600 Pennsylvania Ave., Washington, DC • 202-208-1631 • www.nps.gov/whho

## » Fort Norfolk and Fort Monroe National Monument

The city of Norfolk, Virginia, is at the center of Hampton Roads, at the mouth of the Chesapeake Bay. In 1794, George Washington ordered **Fort Norfolk** to be built overlooking the Elizabeth River. In June 1813, it faced the prospect of a British raid, but was spared when 750 Americans, including crew from the U.S.S. *Constellation* (see p. 106) fought off the attack at the Battle of Craney Island. The fort's **dungeons** and **barracks** are open for inspection.

After the War of 1812, new coastal forts were built, including **Fort Monroe.** Its **Casemate Museum** displays weaponry and costumes. Nearby, **Old Point Comfort Lighthouse,** built in 1802, was occupied by the British during the war.

Fort Norfolk, 801 Front St., Norfolk, VA • 757-640-1720 • www.norfolkhistorical.org • Closed Sept. to May (open weekends only June to Aug.); Fort Monroe, 41 Bernard Rd., Hampton, VA • 757-788-3391 (Casemate Museum: 757-722-3678) • www.nps.gov/fomr

### Quick History

When the British invaded Washington in 1814, President James Madison was away inspecting military preparations, leaving First Lady Dolley Madison in charge of the President's House. Before fleeing, Dolley, aided by the slave Paul Jennings, removed state papers and other valuables, including the portrait of George Washington by Gilbert Stuart, today hanging in the East Room. While the White House was rebuilt, Dolley and the President moved to the Octagon House at 1799 New York Avenue Northwest. It was here that the President signed the Treaty of Ghent, which ended the war.

## ›› STAR-SPANGLED BANNER NATIONAL HISTORIC TRAIL

As a commercial hub and a center of government, the Chesapeake Bay area was a target for the British in the War of 1812. The Star-Spangled Banner National Historic Trail follows the movements of British troops, by land and water, as they traveled inland and upriver, encountering U.S. troops and civilians hundreds of times over a two-year period. The trail links national historic landmarks, state parks, National Park Service sites, and Washington—where the original Star-Spangled Banner that flew above Fort McHenry (see p. 110) is now on display—with Baltimore, where Francis Scott Key was inspired to write the lyrics that later became the U.S. national anthem.

**Fell's Point** Originally a separate settlement founded in 1730, Fell's Point is now a vibrant part of Baltimore. Its cobblestoned waterfront is lined with late 18th- and early 19th-century buildings. During the War of 1812 the town was a base for American privateers paid to attack British shipping. Baltimore clippers built in the shipyards of Fell's Point also helped transport munitions and other supplies to the American troops, often dodging the British naval blockade. In April each year Fell's Point celebrates Privateer Day.

**Baltimore, MD • www.fellspoint.us**

### Site Specific

✴ **TRAIL MAP** Learn more about the Star-Spangled Banner Trail, download a map of the 560-mile (900 km) route, and plan your visit at www.starspangledtrail.net. Look for orientation kiosks at more than 25 locations en route. Or download the Chesapeake Explorer App to explore sites, activities, and itineraries.

**U.S.S. *Constellation*** Though its masts are dwarfed by downtown Baltimore's skyline, the U.S.S. *Constellation,* permanently docked at the Inner Harbor's Pier One, remains a proud reminder of the age of fighting sailing ships. This ship is not, however, the original *Constellation,* which was built in Baltimore in 1797 and became one of the U.S. Navy's most famous ships (even if it had to sit out the War of 1812 blockaded in Norfolk, Virginia). The current ship is a sloop of war that was launched in 1854 and given the name *Constellation* in honor of its illustrious predecessor. It is thought to incorporate hull material from the original ship.

Also sometimes in dock is the ***Pride of Baltimore II,*** a reproduction of a Baltimore clipper, the schooner favored by U.S. privateers during the war. The ship sails the world as a goodwill ambassador, but is occasionally open for public events.

**Constellation Dock, Inner Harbor at Pier 1, 301 East Pratt St., Baltimore, MD • www .historicships.org/constellation.html**

Francis Scott Key, author of the lyrics to "The Star-Spangled Banner"

**U.S. Naval Academy** Thirty miles (48 km) south of Baltimore, the U.S. Naval Academy in Annapolis was established in 1845 on the site of Fort Severn, built to protect Annapolis during the war (though it never saw action). A **museum** at the academy exhibits numerous 1812 artifacts, including U.S. Commodore Oliver Hazard Perry's "Don't Give Up the Ship" flag, made to inspire U.S. sailors going into battle, and the British Royal Standard taken at Fort York (see pp. 60–62). Annapolis's **visitor center** issues leaflets detailing self-guided tours of the town and costumed interpreters conduct guided walks. In summer, boat tours with an 1812 theme depart from City Dock.

**U.S. Naval Academy Museum, Preble Hall, 118 Maryland Ave., Annapolis, MD • 410-293-2108 • www.usna.edu/museum; visitor center, 26 West St., Annapolis, MD • 410-280-0444 • www.visitannapolis.org**

**Bladensburg Battlefield** The residential neighborhood of Bladensburg was the site of one of the most famous battles of the war. To find out about the hot afternoon of August 24, 1814, when British Regulars routed the hastily assembled U.S. forces and entered Washington, head for the **Battle of Bladensburg Visitor Center,** overlooking the Anacostia River in Bladensburg Waterfront Park. Rosalie Stier Calvert witnessed the battle from **Riversdale House,** a federal mansion that is now a museum. Calvert's family purportedly entertained wounded British troops here. Guided tours of the property take place on Friday and Sunday afternoon.

About a mile and a half (2.4 km) to the west of the visitor center, in **Fort Lincoln Cemetery,** stands a marker commemorating the 500 American seamen and marines who, commanded by Commodore Joshua

Barney, courageously stood their ground near this spot, delaying the British advance with cannon, cutlasses, and pikes. The grassy slopes of the cemetery are dotted with ancient oaks, looking very much as they might have done in 1814.

**Battle of Bladensburg Visitor Center, 4601 Annapolis Rd., Bladensburg, MD • 301-927-8819 • www.battleofbladensburg1812.com; Fort Lincoln Cemetery, 3401 Bladensburg Rd., Brentwood, MD • 301-864-5090 • www.fort-lincoln.com**

### National Museum of American History

The most famous American flag, the one that Francis Scott Key glimpsed flying above Baltimore's Fort McHenry on September 14, 1814 (see pp. 110–111), is on display at the Smithsonian's National Museum of American History. Called **"The Star-Spangled Banner: The Flag that Inspired the National Anthem,"** the exhibit showcases the 30-by-34-foot (9 by 10 m) icon lying at a ten-degree angle in suitably dim light. The flag was one of two banners commissioned for Fort McHenry from Mary Pickersgill, a Baltimore widow who earned money making ships' colors.

The banner, which has undergone conservation, is flanked by galleries relating the story of the flag, the bombardment of Fort McHenry, and how Scott Key's lyrics became the national anthem.

**1300 Constitution Avenue, N.W., Washington, D.C. • 202-633-1000 • www.americanhistory.si.edu**

In spring and summer visitors to the National Museum of American History can participate in folding a full-size copy of the Star-Spangled Banner.

## Oxon Hill Farm and Oxon Cove Park

An early 19th-century plantation, **Oxon Hill Farm** overlooks the Potomac River, a few miles downstream from Washington. **Mount Welby,** the two-story plantation house, commissioned by the owner, Dr. Samuel DeButts, was completed in 1811—a year before the war erupted.

In August 1814, as a British fleet approached Alexandria, Virginia, the DeButts family evacuated their new home. While they were away three Congreve rockets, fired by a British ship sending signals to the British fleet in the Patuxent River 20 miles (32 km) away, devastated the property.

Today, Oxon Hill is a National Park Service working farm. Its outbuildings re-create plantation life around the Chesapeake Bay at the time of the War of 1812. In **Oxon Cove Park,** surrounding the farm, visitors can help with farm chores, take a wagon ride, and walk along the riverside.

**6411 Oxon Hill Rd., Oxon Hill, MD • 301-839-1176 • www.nps.gov/oxhi**

**Fort Washington Park** Rising on a promontory 12 miles (19 km) southeast of Alexandria, Virginia, **Fort Washington** was built to protect the nation's capital from invaders sailing upriver. Then called Fort Warburton, it was completed in 1809. Five years later, in August 1814, Fort Warburton faced danger. Seven British warships approached along the Potomac while British land forces marched on Washington. Three days after the British torched the capital (see p. 105), British troops arriving at Fort Warburton found it destroyed by its own garrison. The British had hardly departed before rebuilding began. A new fort rose from the ashes in 1824.

Occasional **historical reenactments** take place in the grounds. Visitors can also explore trails and use picnic facilities with views over the Potomac River.

**13551 Fort Washington Rd., Fort Washington, MD • 301-763-1389 • www.nps.gov/oxhi • $**

**Jefferson Patterson Park and Museum** In June 1814 Commodore Joshua Barney, an ex-privateer attempted to break the British hold on the Chesapeake Bay. Assembling a fleet of old gunboats and barges called the Cheaspeake Bay Flotilla, he launched a series of attacks, including one on St. Leonard's Creek on the Calvert Peninsula. From Jefferson Park on the shore of the creek, a U.S. battery was trained on British forces. Cannonballs have been found here.

The **visitor center** exhibit, "Farmers, Patriots, and Traitors," explores the history of the campaign, and there is an 1812-themed audio tour. Other attractions include hiking trails and a re-created Indian village. ∎

**10515 Mackall Rd., St. Leonard, MD • 410-586-8501 • www.jefpat.org • Visitor Center closed Sun. to Tue. and mid-Oct. to mid-April**

### Nearby & Noteworthy

✱ **CALVERT MARINE MUSEUM** Exhibits include an electronic map of British troop movements up the Patuxent River and artifacts recovered from a U.S. Chesapeake Bay Flotilla vessel scuttled in the river. *14200 Soloman Islands Rd. Solomons, MD, www.calvertmarinemuseum.com*

✱ **SOTTERLEY PLANTATION** This plantation was raided by British troops during the war. It offers War of 1812 lectures and activities as well as riverside walks and gardens. *Sotterley Ln., Hollywood, MD, www.sotterley.org*

## » Fort McHenry National Monument and Historic Shrine

Fort McHenry is on Locust Point, a peninsula jutting out into the Patapsco River. Erected in 1798 to protect Baltimore city, it served as its primary guardian for more than a century. Named after James McHenry, Secretary of War under George Washington, the fort takes the shape of a five-pointed star and is surrounded by a dry moat. The angles formed by the star made taking the fort a formidable challenge since they enabled the fort's defenders to lay down crossfire on any attackers. The fort came under enemy attack only once during its history.

In 1814, the British attempted to raid Baltimore and destroy shipping in its harbor, but 22 U.S. vessels sunk to block the harbor entrance meant that the British had to invade by land and destroy Fort McHenry first. Beginning at 6 a.m. on September 13, their warships bombarded Fort McHenry for 25 hours. Nearly 2,000 exploding bombs were launched at the fort, killing four people. While under heavy bombardment, the American defenders determinedly returned fire with cannon.

Thanks to the steadfastness of the fort's garrison, the sturdiness of its design, and the sunken ships across the harbor's entrance, the British failed to advance. Unwilling to risk severe damage to their ships, the British broke off the attack and withdrew down the Patapsco River.

**Fort McHenry commemorates the Battle for Baltimore on the anniversary of the battle and offers regular talks and events, including hands-on activities such as artillery drill, throughout the year.**

The Star-Spangled Banner continued to fly over the fort. The sight inspired Francis Scott Key, a U.S. lawyer and amateur poet negotiating the release of a U.S. prisoner

aboard a truce ship off Baltimore at the time, to pen the lines that were later adapted for "The Star-Spangled Banner." Meanwhile, the British land attack on Baltimore was repulsed at North Point and Hampstead Hill. By September 15, the British had decided to retreat from the area, leaving Baltimore safely in American hands.

**The fort today** After World War I, Fort McHenry was restored to look as it did in the 19th century and turned over to the National Park Service in 1933. Today, a reproduction of the famous Star-Spangled Banner still flies over the fort (the original is in the National Museum of American History; see p. 108). Easily accessible from Baltimore Harbor by water taxi, the historic site is set on more than 40 acres (16 ha) of parkland. A mile-long (2 km) **loop trail** passes two groves of trees planted in memory of the battle and a statue of Orpheus honoring Francis Scott Key.

At the **visitor center** near the entrance to the site, visitors can see an orientation film and interactive exhibits. Next, follow the pathway toward the fort itself, which

The five points of the star-shaped Fort McHenry are clearly visible in this aerial photograph.

and the city of Baltimore. Outside the fort's walls is the **Rodman Battery,** a virtually unparalleled collection of Civil War-era cannon.

**Raising the flag** During the summer months, visitors can take part in the raising or lowering of a copy of the fort's huge Stars and Stripes. The process requires 60 people to take part. Maj. George Armistead, the fort's commanding officer, commissioned the original supersized flag from Mary Pickersgill (see p. 108), so that "the British will have

goes past the Water Battery, an exhibit highlighting the guns that fended off the British in 1814.

Inside the fort, **exhibits** tell 200 years of the fort's history with items recovered from archaeological digs at the fort, as well as weapons, flags, photographs, and rare documents. Visitors can follow the progress of the fighting as it happened in September 1814 using an electronic battle map. Original buildings, including the **commander's and enlisted men's quarters,** as well as the **guardhouse** and **powder magazine,** form part of the museum.

From the walls of the fort, there are far-reaching views over the Patapsco River

no difficulty seeing it from a distance." As well as making the large garrison flag, Mary Pickersgill also made a smaller flag for use during storms. Because the copy flag is so large, it can only be flown safely if the wind speed is between 5 and 12 miles per hour (8–20 kph).

Each year on the second Saturday in September, Baltimore celebrates Defenders' Day, commemorating the 1814 victory. It is a state holiday in which Fort McHenry plays a central role, with parades, fireworks, and historical reenactments.

**2400 East Fort Ave., Baltimore, MD • 410-962-4290 • www.nps.gov/fomc • $**

## » *Other Sites & Plaques*

✤ *Annapolis Royal Historic District National Historic Site* This beautifully restored town preserves many early 19th-century buildings, including Fort Anne. **St. George St., Annapolis Royal, NS • www.parkscanada.gc.ca**

✤ *Castle Hill National Historic Site* During the War of 1812, the British occupied this site overlooking Placentia Bay. Remnants of French fortifications, a blockhouse, and cannon remain. **Castle Hill Rd., off Route 100, Placentia, NL • www.parkscanada.gc.ca**

✤ *Fort Beauséjour National Historic Site* Reinforced by the British during the War of 1812, this was the first pentagonal fort in North America. Visitors can explore the ramparts and soldiers' barracks. **111 Fort Beauséjour Rd., Aulac, NB • www.parkscanada.gc.ca**

✤ *Fort Howe National Historic Site* The City of St. John, New Brunswick, now surrounds the site of Fort Howe, a British fortification on the mouth of the Saint John River. A cairn and plaque mark the spot. **Saint John, NB • www.parkscanada.gc.ca**

★ *Fort Sewall, Essex National Heritage Area* In 1814, Fort Sewall provided cannon cover for the U.S.S. *Constitution* (see p. 100). In summer, Revolutionary War reenactors showcase colonial crafts and activities. **Front St., Marblehead, MA • 978-740-0444• www.essexheritage.org**

★ *Fort Wadsworth* Guarding the entrance to New York Harbor, this fort formed part of a larger defense system. There are good views of New York from the battlements. **210 New York Ave., Staten Island, NY • 718-354-4500 • www.nps.gov/gate**

★ *Friendship Hill National Historic Site* Albert Gallatin, Secretary of the Treasury during the War of 1812, built his home, Friendship Hill, in western Pennsylvania. Gallatin believed the war "renewed and reinstated the national feeling and character." **Point Marion, PA • www.nps.gov/frhi**

★ *John H. Chafee Blackstone River Valley National Heritage Corridor* In 1807, Congress passed the Embargo Act in retaliation for British and French disruption to U.S. shipping. With the supply of British textiles cut off, cotton production expanded in the Blackstone Valley. The route goes through 24 towns, including Pawtucket, Rhode Island, which has the oldest surviving factory in the U.S. **• 401-762-0250 • www.nps.gov/blac**

✤ *Old Town Lunenburg National Historic Site* Among Lunenburg's original 18th-century buildings are a parade square and waterfront houses. **Lunenburg, NS • www.parkscanada.gc.ca**

★ *Springfield Armory National Historic Site* The Model 1812 musket was developed in Springfield. Although not ready in time for the war, it later became standard issue for U.S. infantry. **One Armory Sq., Springfield, MA • 413-734-8551 • www.nps.gov/spar**

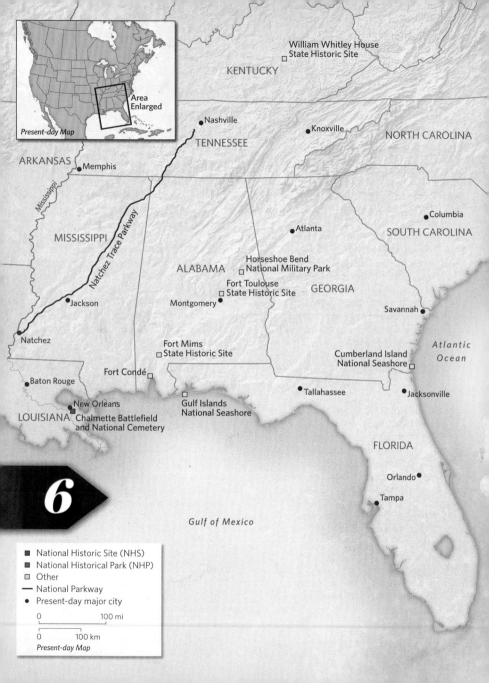

William Whitley House
State Historic Site

KENTUCKY

Nashville
TENNESSEE
Knoxville

NORTH CAROLINA

ARKANSAS
Memphis

Mississippi

Natchez Trace Parkway

MISSISSIPPI

Columbia
SOUTH CAROLINA

Atlanta

ALABAMA
Horseshoe Bend
National Military Park

Jackson

Fort Toulouse
State Historic Site
GEORGIA

Montgomery

Savannah

Natchez

Fort Mims
State Historic Site

Atlantic
Ocean

Fort Condé
Cumberland Island
National Seashore

Baton Rouge

New Orleans
LOUISIANA Chalmette Battlefield
and National Cemetery

Gulf Islands
National Seashore

Tallahassee
Jacksonville

FLORIDA

Orlando
Tampa

**6**

Gulf of Mexico

■ National Historic Site (NHS)
■ National Historical Park (NHP)
□ Other
— National Parkway
• Present-day major city

0        100 mi

0        100 km

*Present-day Map*

Present-day Map
Area
Enlarged

# THE SOUTHEAST

The war was slow to arrive in the Southeast, even though people had anticipated it since the start. Most people expected it to come in the form of a British fleet off the Gulf Coast. A successful British attack on New Orleans, in concert with a war against those Native groups who were resisting American encroachment into their territories, and perhaps a slave uprising, might have entailed the loss of the Louisiana Territory, or worse.

In summer 1813, a civil war within the Creek Nation (see pp. 15–16) engulfed the entire region. Had there been no Creek War, the U.S. command would have stripped the Southeast of men and resources to feed the Canadian front. As it was, when the British arrived off the Gulf Coast in late 1814, they faced an experienced U.S. army. The battle for New Orleans would eventually propel a general named Andrew Jackson into the White House.

**An illustration of Menawa, Creek chief and leader of the Red Sticks during the Battle of Horseshoe Bend**

# » HORSESHOE BEND NATIONAL MILITARY PARK

In March 1814, east-central Alabama was so remote that Maj. Gen. Andrew Jackson, at the head of 2,600 U.S. regulars and Tennessee militiamen and a further 600 Native warriors, mostly Cherokee, had to cut a 52-mile (84 km) trail through the forest to reach the spot where the Tallapoosa River curls back on itself. At the base of the fortified peninsula formed by the bend in the river stood Tohopeka, the last stronghold of the Red Sticks faction of the Creek Nation. Today's park preserves the site of the final battle of the Creek War of 1813–1814 (see box p. 117).

At about 10 a.m. on March 27, Jackson's army reached the Overlook, a prominent hill at the northern end of the peninsula formed by Horseshoe Bend. The hill, where a marked route round the battlefield begins (allow two hours if driving, three if walking), provides a sweeping view down a grassy plain toward a distant row of white stakes that marked the position of what was the battlefield's most prominent landmark: the Red Sticks' log barricade. Long vanished now, it was made of giant pine trees and stretched some 400 yards (365 m) from one side of the peninsula to the other. More

than 5 feet (1.5 m) tall, it was angled to channel an attacking force into a crossfire. Behind this obstacle stood nearly a thousand Red Sticks warriors waiting for the attack.

**U.S. bombardment** Farther along the route, a **cannon** stands beside a **monument** placed by Congress in 1918 (and bearing the wrong date!). This is the approximate position of Jackson's two artillery pieces—a

**Horseshoe Bend in the Tallapoosa River. During the battle, Cherokee warriors led American forces across the river to attack the Red Sticks from behind.**

3-pounder and a 6-pounder—which at about 10:30 "opened a brisk fire." They pounded away at those logs for two hours, but did comparatively little damage. Then Jackson called for a bayonet charge.

His infantry, beating their drums, marched down the plain into a hail of musket balls and arrows. Along the line marked by those white stakes, a fierce battle raged—it was "muzzle to muzzle through the portholes," Jackson later wrote. Yet the soldiers, with numbers and firepower on their side, were soon pouring over the barricade.

**Attack across the river** Further stops along the route explain why the general ordered that frontal charge. Before the battle, Jackson had sent his mounted riflemen and Native auxiliaries across the Tallapoosa to encircle the "horseshoe." Stop Number Three marks the spot where Cherokee warriors swam the river to the Red Sticks side and began burning Tohopeka, the Red Sticks village. (A trail leads to a shelter overlooking the site.) Seeing the smoke and guessing its meaning, Jackson pressed home his advantage.

The carnage that resulted that afternoon, as Jackson later admitted to his wife, was "*dreadful*." Though most of the 350 Creek women and children were taken captive, the Red Sticks warriors, the vise tightening around them, were ruthlessly hunted down and killed. After darkness fell, perhaps a couple of dozen Red Sticks—including their wounded chief, Menawa—escaped by canoe. Jackson buried his own 49 dead in the river and moved on.

**The battle site today** Two centuries have now passed, and some 70,000 visitors a year stroll through the park's 2,040 rolling acres (825 ha) of woods and meadows. The park

## Quick History

The Creek War of 1813–1814 was rooted in a schism between those members of the Creek confederacy—as white Americans called the assemblage of interrelated tribes living in present-day Georgia and Alabama—who were giving up the old ways and adopting European customs, and those who deplored such developments, hoping instead to protect their lands and purge the white man's influence.

The traditionalists were called Red Sticks because they wielded red-painted war clubs. Outside of their victory at Fort Mims in August 1813 (see pp. 120–121), the Red Sticks suffered one defeat after another. They had few guns and little powder or shot. And in less than a year after Fort Mims, U.S. forces had destroyed most of their towns, leaving their women and children to starve. The lasting animosities generated by the war ultimately led to the Indian Removals of the 1830s, those Trails of Tears that saw nearly all of the Southeastern Native Nations exiled west of the Mississippi.

has become a place of national reconciliation and remembrance, commemorating the largest loss of Native warriors' lives in any single battle with U.S. forces. The battle is commemorated in March with living history and artillery displays and anniversary observances. At other times, visitors can follow the tour road around the battle site, hike, fish, and picnic. ∎

**11288 Horseshoe Bend Rd., Daviston, AL • 256-234-7111 • www.nps.gov/hobe**

## ›› *Chalmette Battlefield and National Cemetery*

**Hemmed in by man and nature, Chalmette Battlefield and National Cemetery in Jean Lafitte National Historical Park and Preserve is one of the most storied pieces of American soil. On January 8, 1815, Maj. Gen. Andrew Jackson's force won a decisive victory over an imposing British army at Chalmet plantation outside New Orleans in the last major land battle of the war. The "Glorious Eighth" of January was soon being hailed as the greatest American land victory of the war.**

Gone are the cypress swamps and acres of sugarcane of the early 1800s. Gone, too, is the ground that once supported Jackson's right flank, washed away by the changing course of the Mississippi River. The only man-made battlefield feature that remains is the Rodriguez Canal, then a major obstacle running the length of Jackson's defensive line, now reduced to a shallow depression.

Across these fields, at dawn on January 8, 1815, came 7,000 seasoned British infantrymen in the climactic assault of a three-week campaign to capture New Orleans, key to the Mississippi River Valley and hence to the North American heartland. Facing them behind that

canal and an earthen rampart were 4,000 U.S. soldiers, including Choctaw warriors. Neither the attacking English, Scottish, and West Indian troops, nor the waiting Kentucky, Tennessee, and Louisiana militiamen knew that 15 days earlier a peace treaty had been agreed that would end the war that had brought them to this spot—for the ships bearing news of the Treaty of Ghent (see box) were still struggling across the Atlantic.

Instead, the American batteries roared into life and a sheet of flame erupted from their massed muskets and rifles. Within two hours, the battle was over. Fewer than 20 Americans were dead, wounded, or captured. The British suffered more than 2,000 casualties including the death of their commander, Maj. Gen. Sir Edward Pakenham, the Duke of Wellington's brother-in-law.

**Chalmette today** In 2005 Chalmette Battlefield was devastated by Hurricane Katrina. Since then, it has been restored, and from behind the partially reconstructed American rampart silent cannon point across green fields where Spanish moss festoons the live oak trees. In early January

**A 19th-century print of the Battle of New Orleans shows British soldiers fighting as officers aid the wounded General Pakenham.**

## Quick History

On December 24, 1814, in the medieval city of Ghent, in what is today Belgium, diplomats from the United Kingdom and the United States signed a peace treaty. Behind-the-scenes maneuvering had long been under way, but the two delegations did not confer face to face until August 1814. Four months of parleying ended with the two war-weary nations agreeing only to return to the state of affairs existing before hostilities began. The "Peace of Christmas Eve" would not come into force until ratified by both sides. This happened quickly in London, but it was February 1815 before a ship could bring the Treaty of Ghent to Washington.

each year buckskinned Tennesseans, Kentucky riflemen, U.S. Army regulars in tall shakos, Jean Lafitte's dashing Baratarian pirates, and New Orleans' own free men of color commemorate the battle. Redcoats and tartan-clad Highlanders make their battle plans, and the smoke of black powder drifts over the scene. The annual event draws living history enthusiasts from all over the U.S. and Canada.

Situated next to the **Chalmette Monument** (a 100-foot/30 m obelisk begun in 1840 but not completed until 1908 under the auspices of the U.S. Daughters of 1812), the new visitor center features films, exhibits, displays of period weapons, and an interactive map depicting the troop movements that led up to the battle. Wayside signs on the battlefield describe the battle and share the land's story in the years that followed. The **National Cemetery** along the battlefield's eastern edges dates from the Civil War. The dead from that conflict account for most of its 15,000 graves, though soldiers from the Revolutionary War through Vietnam are also buried there, including four from the War of 1812. ■

8606 West St. Bernard Hwy., Chalmette, LA • 504-281-0510 • www.nps.gov/jela/chalmette-battlefield.htm

## ›› *Natchez Trace Parkway*

Originally a trail scraped out by the hooves of migrating bison, then worn into a smooth footpath by generations of Chickasaw and Choctaw, the Natchez Trace meandered hundreds of miles across the ridges joining the lower Mississippi River with Tennessee's Nashville Basin. By the early 19th century, it had become a thoroughfare studded with inns and trading posts and served a colorful cavalcade of farmers, frontiersmen, trappers, gamblers, preachers, highwaymen, Chickasaw, Choctaw, and, during the War of 1812, marching Tennessee militiamen.

Today visitors can follow this legendary route, either driving the scenic, 444-mile (715 km) Natchez Trace Parkway or hiking the intertwined Natchez Trace National Scenic Trail. Most of the militiamen began at Nashville, where a new **monument** at Milepost 426.3 honors "the services of all brave volunteers" who marched on the Trace during that conflict—the most famous being Gen. Andrew Jackson, commander of the Tennessee Militia. In January 1813, Jackson moved his men down to Washington, outside Natchez, Mississippi. Though his infantry floated down the Mississippi on flatboats, his cavalry rode down the Trace. Off Milepost 407.7 you can see the **home of Capt. John Gordon,** commander of Jackson's "spies," or mounted scouts.

Three months later, Jackson's troops were disbanded. Though many were hungry and sick, they all slogged up the Trace, through pouring rain, hailstorms, and knee-deep mud. Jackson went every step of the six-week journey with them. His men, recognizing in their wiry, whip-lean general an admirable resilience, gave him a lasting nickname—"Old Hickory."

After the Battle of New Orleans, volunteer militiamen returned north on the Natchez Trace, now a National Scenic Trail.

Visitors can explore many parts of the old Trace along which the volunteers marched. At the **Sunken Trace** (Milepost 41.5), there is a picturesque stretch sunk deep between banks of earth. At **Colbert Ferry** (Milepost 327.3), where travelers crossed the broad Tennessee River, there once stood an inn. On the night of March 23, 1815, one southbound traveler staying there complained in his diary of the noise being made by U.S. soldiers returning from New Orleans—soldiers celebrating the news that the war was finally over.

**Natchez Trace Parkway visitor center, Milepost 266, Tupelo, MS • 800-305-7417 • www.nps.gov/natr**

## ›› *Fort Mims State Historic Site*

"Remember Fort Mims!" rang throughout the country in the months following an attack on the fort by Red Sticks Creeks in retaliation for the Battle of Burnt Corn Creek, an ambush on a party of Red Sticks

Anticipating a Red Stick attack, Mississippi Territorial militia hurriedly fortified the plantation of Samuel Mims, where Americans—many of Creek descent—had gathered for protection. Among the 400 people crowded into the stockade were white planters, their African slaves, around 100 militiamen, as well as Creeks opposed to the Red Sticks movement.

Around 700 Red Sticks warriors emerged from the woods around noon that late summer day and stormed the fort. Five hours later they left it a smoking ruin, having taken most of the slaves captive but killing nearly everyone else—some 250–300 people, including many women and children. Only a handful had escaped.

Today panels and kiosks on an **interpretive walkway** relate the story, and there is an audio recording in the entrance pavilion. In August a commemoration takes place, and the 5 acres (2 ha) become crowded with living history displays.

Cty. Rte. 80 W, Tensaw, AL • 251-937-5710
• www.preserveala.org

warriors by U.S. militia and Creeks opposed to the Red Sticks movement. The attack on Fort Mims brought the U.S. into open conflict with the Red Sticks.

After the war the site was plowed over, abandoned, and forgotten. It is unmistakable now, however, thanks to the joint efforts of the Alabama Historical Commission and the Fort Mims Restoration Association. A reconstruction of a **frontier stockade** rears out of the woods some 35 miles (56 km) north of Mobile. Archaeological studies began here in the 1950s, and careful excavations have since revealed much about what really happened on that fateful August 30, 1813.

## Quick History

No one embodied the divided loyalties of the Creek War as did William Weatherford (1780–1824), son of a Scots trader and a Creek mother. Weatherford—sometimes called Red Eagle—was a planter and slave owner who became a Red Sticks commander. He even led the attack on Fort Mims that resulted in the killing of some of his own relatives. And once the war was truly lost, he rode boldly into Jackson's camp and surrendered in person. Old Hickory, impressed, spared his life—and the two men soon became friends.

## » FORT TOULOUSE STATE HISTORIC SITE

In the 1770s, when naturalist William Bartram arrived at the confluence of the Coosa and Tallapoosa Rivers in what today is central Alabama, he thought the spot fit for a city. All around him was evidence that other people had long cherished similar ideas, including a prominent burial mound (dating from around A.D. 1100–1400) and the ruins of Fort Toulouse, built by the French and abandoned by them in 1763 when France lost the French and Indian War.

The tree-covered Mississippian mound is still there today. But the French fort has disappeared, as has the Creek village of Taskigi, which was built atop its ruins. In the spring of 1814, fresh from his victory at Horseshoe Bend (see pp. 116–117), Gen. Andrew Jackson and his army arrived there, having torched scores of Creek towns along the way. He swept Taskigi away and raised an American fort on the site—Fort Jackson, his officers called it—and it was there, on August 9, 1814, that he forced upon his defeated and starving foe the Treaty of Fort Jackson, under which the Creek ceded 22 million acres (nearly 9 million ha)—almost half of their territory—to the U.S. Jackson also exacted land cessions from his Creek and Cherokee allies.

Thanks to the Alabama Historical Commission, visitors see a **reconstructed Fort Jackson** today, its grass-covered ramparts bristling with sharpened stakes. Several hundred yards away, near the site's entrance, re-created **Fort Toulouse** has a stockade lined with cannon enclosing barracks and a blacksmith shop.

Hardly a month passes without some kind of living history demonstration in the park, ranging from depictions of the Creek inhabitants to those of a U.S. Army garrison in 1814. There are Frontier Days in the fall and a French and Indian encampment in spring.

A boardwalk called the **William Bartram Trail** winds through 30 acres (12 ha) of forests and fields down to the confluence of the two rivers.

2521 West Fort Toulouse Rd., Wetumpka, AL • 334-567-3002 • www .forttoulouse.com

---

### Quick History

**W**hen he was 13 years old, Andrew Jackson joined a South Carolina militia unit and fought in the Revolutionary War. He carried the scars left by a British saber for the rest of his life.

Although Jackson became a lawyer, businessman, judge, and politician, underneath it all this child of the frontier remained the born fighter, the boy with the cold blue eyes and hair-trigger temper, the brawler, gambler, and duelist.

Forty-five when the War of 1812 began, Old Hickory proved to be a tough and able leader and a ruthless tactician. His victory over the Red Sticks at Horseshoe Bend in 1814 and his unlikely defeat of a large British force near New Orleans the following January made him a national figure. He was appointed provisional governor of newly acquired Florida in 1821 largely on the strength of having illegally invaded it several times. Jackson was wildly popular in the South and West, and those states ensured that in 1828 he was elected the seventh president of the United States.

## » CUMBERLAND ISLAND NATIONAL SEASHORE

In 1783, the live oak trees growing on this wave-lashed spot off Georgia attracted Revolutionary War hero Nathanael Greene. The gnarled, evergreen live oak was the finest shipbuilding timber in the world. Greene died in 1786, never knowing that Cumberland Island live oak timbers would form the hull of the U.S.S. *Constitution*—"Old Ironsides" (see pp. 100–101)—the frigate that won its nickname during the War of 1812.

Greene also left his widow to complete Dungeness, a house overlooking the island's southern marshes. In the first two months of 1815, after British forces had invaded the island, Adm. Sir George Cockburn commandeered the house as his temporary headquarters. The house burned to the ground in 1866, and the ruins of Dungeness that today's visitors gaze upon are mainly those of a later house built on the site, which also succumbed to fire in 1959. However, the remnants of a four-story tabby house on the grounds date from Greene's tenure.

When Cockburn arrived on the island in early 1815—after the treaty but before notice reached the U.S.—many enslaved African Americans volunteered for service in response to British promises to grant slaves their freedom if they served the British cause. In 1815, U.S. commissioners informed the British of the treaty ratification and demanded the return of their property. Many black volunteers were returned to slavery.

Cockburn also occupied St. Marys—having first destroyed its guardian fort on adjacent Point Peter, the forested peninsula that the ferry passes as it crosses between the town and the island. Artifacts found at the site of that long-vanished fort are now displayed in the **Cumberland Island Museum** in St. Marys, which has devoted an entire room to the War of 1812.

Admiral Cockburn did not long remain in his new quarters. When word came of the Treaty of Ghent, which ended the war, his fleet sailed away, dropping former slaves off in Trinidad to start a new life in freedom.

**St. Marys, GA • 912-882-4336 • www.nps.gov/cuis • $**

**The current ruins of Dungeness mark the site of the house used by Admiral Cockburn.**

## ›› *Other Sites & Plaques*

★ *Fort Bowyer* Today Fort Morgan stands on the site of Fort Bowyer, which fell to the British in the last land battle of the war. A plaque on the grounds of Fort Morgan marks the spot where the original fort stood. **Off Ala. 180, Fort Morgan, AL • 251-540-5257 • www .fortmorgan.org**

★ *Fort Condé* In April 1813, when Gen. James Wilkinson captured Mobile, the Stars and Stripes became the fourth flag raised over what the British called Fort Charlotte, the Spanish Fort Carlotta, and the French had christened Fort Condé. The newly renovated fort houses exhibits on Mobile's colonial history. **150 South Royal St., Mobile, AL • 251-208-7569 • www.museumofmobile.com**

★ *Fort Gadsden Historic Site* Overlooking the Apalachicola River are the remains of a British fort built in 1814 in what was then Spanish Florida. After the war it became a haven for run-away slaves and in 1816 American forces crossed the border and destroyed it. **Apalachicola Ranger District 11152, NW Fla. 20, Bristol, FL • 850-643-2282 • www .fs.usda.gov/florida**

★ *Fort Gaines* In 1816, the U.S. Army erected a log stockade on a bluff above the Chattahoochee River on lands ceded by the Creek Nation in the Treaty of Fort Jackson. Today a park preserves the site and features reconstructed period buildings. **Bluff St., Fort Gaines, GA • 229-768-2248 • www .fortgaines.com**

★ *Fort Mitchell Historic Site* A reconstructed log palisade and a visitor center mark the site where, in 1813, U.S. troops built Fort Mitchell as a bulwark against Red Sticks Creeks. In the 1830s, the Creek Nation marched into exile from here, across the Mississippi River. The Chattahoochee Indian Heritage Center is across the road. **561 Ala. 165, Fort Mitchell, AL • 334-855-1406**

★ *Gulf Islands National Seashore* When Andrew Jackson marched on Pensacola in late 1814, the British quickly evacuated Fort Barrancas. Its "water battery" remains largely unchanged today. The British fleet anchored off Ship Island, on the National Seashore's other side, during the New Orleans campaign. **1801 Gulf Breeze Pkwy., Gulf Breeze, FL • 850-455-5167 • www.nps.gov/guis**

★ *Virgin Islands National Park* Out of the cactus scrub on Hassel Island rear the imposing ruins of Fort Willoughby, Cowell's Battery, and Shipley's Battery, all occupied by British troops during the war to protect Britain's Caribbean trade. **1300 Cruz Bay Creek, St. John, VI • 340-776-6201 • www.nps.gov/viis**

★ *William Whitley House State Historic Site* A rifle that might have killed Tecumseh is on display at William Whitley House with other artifacts from the 1813 Battle of the Thames (see p. 28). Whether he shot the Shawnee leader or not, Whitley was also mortally wounded. **625 William Whitley Rd., Stanford, KY • 606-355-2881**

# >> INDEX

## Authors
Mark Collins Jenkins
Jacob F. Field
Michael Kerrigan
Cynthia O'Brien
Joe Yogerst

## Picture credits
**tr = top right**
**Front cover**: Library of Congress, Print & Photographs Division, LC-DIG-pga-01838; **2-3** New York State Office of Parks, Recreation and Historic Sites; **4** Dale Wilson/Parks Canada; **5tr** M.Trépanier/Parks Canada; 5ml Mackinac State Historic Parks; 5br M.Trépanier/Parks Canada; **10** Philadelphia History Museum at Atwater, Kent/Courtesy of Historical Society of Pennsylvania Collection/The Bridgeman Art Library; **13** Library of Congress Prints and Photographs; **14** *Major-General Sir Isaac Brock, KB, George Theodore Berthon*, Archives of Ontario, 694158; **17** Library of Congress Prints and Photographs; **19** © Collection of the New-York Historical Society, USA/The Bridge-man Art Library; **20** Library of Congress Prints and Photographs; **23** Mackinac State Historic Parks; **25** Parks Canada; **27** M.Trépanier/Parks Canada; **29** Brian Morin/Parks Canada; **30-31** Fort Meigs State Memorial; **32** Dan Feicht/Courtesy of Lake Erie Shores & Islands; **34** Monroe County Convention and Tourism Bureau; **35** M.Trépanier/Parks Canada; **36** Ontario Parks; **39** M.Trépanier/Parks Canada; **41** J.Bernard/Parks Canada; **43** Parks Canada; **44-45** Library and Archives of Canada, Acc. No. 1970-188-517 W.H.Coverdale Collection of Canadiana; **46** Wally Stemberger/Shutterstock.com; **48** Battlefield House Museum and Park; **51** Zack Frank/View Portfolio/Shutterstock.com; **53** *General Sir Gordon Drummond, GCB, George Theodore Berthon*, Government of Ontario Art Collection, Archives of Ontario, 693127; **54-55** Image courtesy The Niagara Parks Commission; **56** Library and Archives of Canada, Acc. No. 1983-47-118; **59** City of Toronto, Museum Services, 1986.23.1; **60-61** Library and Archives of Canada, Acc. No. 1990-336-3;

**63** © 2012 Ontario Tourism Marketing Partnership Corporation; **65** Al Fink; **67** Fort Ontario State Historic Site, New York State Office of Parks Recreation and Historic Preservation; **71** Jeffrey M.Frank/Shutterstock.com; **72** Eric Le Bel/Parks Canada; **73** Parks Canada; **74** Municipalité de Saint-Paul-de-l'Île-aux-Noix; **76** Library and Archives of Canada, Acc. No. 1984-164-46, source: Mr. Laurent Allard, Laval, Quebec; **78-79** MBphotography/Shutterstock.com; **81** *Fort Wellington, Prescott, Thomas Burrowes*, Archives of Ontario, C 1-0-0-0-78 (detail); **82-83** © 2012 Ontario Tourism Marketing Partnership Corporation; **84** Ontario Parks; **85** Air Photo Max/Parks Canada; **86-87** Parks Canada; **88** *"The Battle of Lake Champlain,"* Julian Davidson, 1894. War of 1812 Museum, Battle of Plattsburgh Association. 31 Washington Road, Plattsburgh, NY 12901 http://www. battleofplattsburgh.org; **91** Leighton O'Connor/Shutterstock.com; **92-93** Parks Canada; **95** V.J.Matthew/Shutterstock.com; **96-97** Sherab/Alamy; **99** National Park Service; **100** Courtesy Naval Historical Foundation; **103** National Geographic Stock/Michael S. Yamashita; **104** National Park Service; **107** Courtesy of the Maryland Historical Society 1936-17; **108** Courtesy of the Smithsonian's National Museum of American History; **110-111** Alamy/William S. Kuta; **112** National Geographic Stock/Bates Littlehales; **115** Library of Congress Prints and Photographs; **116** National Park Service; **118** Library of Congress Prints and Photographs; **120-121** istockphoto.com/visionsofmaine; **123** National Park Service.

## Acknowledgments
This material is based upon work supported by the New England Interstate Water Pollution Control Commission (NEIWPCC) through a federal cooperative agreement with the National Park Service. National Geographic is also indebted to Parks Canada, the National Park Service, and the Champlain Valley National Heritage Partnership, Lake Champlain Basin Program, and all the individuals who have helped prepare this guide, especially Christine Arato, Ron Dale, Jim Brangan, and John Thomson, as well as Rick Hill, text consultant.

The Champlain Valley National Heritage Partnership is managed by the Lake Champlain Basin Program to conserve, promote, and interpret the rich cultural and natural history of the New York, Quebec, and Vermont communities along the historic Lake Champlain corridor.

**NATIONAL GEOGRAPHIC**

# *1812*
## *A Traveler's Guide*

**CELEBRATING**
# ◄**125**►
**Y E A R S**

### Published by the National Geographic Society
John M. Fahey, *Chairman of the Board and Chief Executive Officer*
Declan Moore, *Executive Vice President; President, Publishing and Travel*
Melina Gerosa Bellows, *Executive Vice President; Chief Creative Officer, Books, Kids, and Family*
Lynn Cutter, *Executive Vice President, Travel*
Keith Bellows, *Senior Vice President and Editor in Chief, National Geographic Travel Media*

### Prepared by the Book Division
Hector Sierra, *Senior Vice President and General Manager*
Janet Goldstein, *Senior Vice President and Editorial Director*
Jonathan Halling, *Design Director, Books and Children's Publishing*
Marianne R. Koszorus, *Design Director, Books*
Barbara A. Noe, *Senior Editor, National Geographic Travel Books*
R. Gary Colbert, *Production Director*
Jennifer A. Thornton, *Director of Managing Editorial*
Susan S. Blair, *Director of Photography*
Meredith C. Wilcox, *Director, Administration and Rights Clearance*

### Staff for This Book
Caroline Hickey, *Project Editor*
Elisa Gibson, Marty Ittner, *Design Consultants*
Carl Mehler, *Director of Maps*
Michael McNey and XNR Productions, *Map Research and Production*
Nancy Marion, *Contributor*
Marshall Kiker, *Associate Managing Editor*
Katie Olsen, *Production Design Assistant*

### Manufacturing and Quality Management
Phillip L. Schlosser, *Senior Vice President*
Chris Brown, *Vice President, NG Book Manufacturing*
George Bounelis, *Vice President, Production Services*
Nicole Elliott, *Manager*
Rachel Faulise, *Manager*
Robert L. Barr, *Manager*

### Created by Toucan Books Ltd
Ellen Dupont, *Editorial Director*
Helen Douglas-Cooper, Dorothy Stannard, *Editors*
Dave Jones, *Designer*
Sharon Southren, *Picture Researcher*
Marion Dent, *Proofreader*
Michael Dent, *Indexer*

The National Geographic Society is one of the world's largest nonprofit scientific and educational organizations. Founded in 1888 to "increase and diffuse geographic knowledge," the Society works to inspire people to care about the planet. National Geographic reflects the world through its magazines, television programs, films, music and radio, books, DVDs, maps, exhibitions, live events, school publishing programs, interactive media and merchandise. *National Geographic* magazine, the Society's official journal, published in English and 33 local-language editions, is read by more than 60 million people each month. The National Geographic Channel reaches 435 million households in 37 languages in 173 countries. National Geographic Digital Media receives more than 19 million visitors a month. National Geographic has funded more than 10,000 scientific research, conservation and exploration projects and supports an education program promoting geography literacy. For more information, visit www.nationalgeographic.com.

For more information, please call 1-800-NGS LINE (647-5463) or write to the following address:

National Geographic Society
1145 17th Street N.W.
Washington, D.C. 20036-4688 U.S.A.

For information about special discounts for bulk purchases, please contact National Geographic Books Special Sales: ngspecsales@ngs.org

For rights or permissions inquiries, please contact National Geographic Books Subsidiary Rights: ngbookrights@ngs.org

ISBN: 978-1-4262-1127-0

Printed in Canada

13/FC/1

The information in this book has been carefully checked and to the best of our knowledge is accurate. However, details are subject to change, and the National Geographic Society cannot be responsible for such changes, or for errors or omissions.